BEYOND
ORGANICS

GARDENING
FOR THE FUTURE

BEYOND ORGANICS

GARDENING
FOR THE FUTURE

HELEN CUSHING

Published by ABC Books for the
AUSTRALIAN BROADCASTING CORPORATION
GPO Box 9994 Sydney NSW 2001

First published April 2005

ISBN 0 7333 1575 5

Designed and typeset by Ellie Exarchos
Typeset in 11/16pt Adobe Caslon
Colour reproduction by Griffin Press
Printed and bound in Australia by Griffin Press
1 3 5 4 2

TO ALL PLANTS, ACROSS ALL TIME,

FOR THEIR INSPIRATION, RESPIRATION

AND TRANSPIRATION — THEY KNOW HOW

TO TRANSFORM LIGHT INTO LIFE.

CONTENTS

ACKNOWLEDGEMENTS

My thanks go to:

All those involved in the production and distribution of tea. I have drunk a plantation in the last 12 months.

Paul, who encouraged, counselled, commented, believed, and whose long-distance presence seemed very close.

Parents, from whom I absorbed eco-consciousness and values that have directed my gaze both outward and inward.

Pippa and Mischa, very patient with their mother's book-writing affliction.

Phil, sharer of the passion for wild nature, who listened to my ramblings in the book's formative years.

Ambikananda, who has a shack overlooking the ocean, which was mine for a week.

Great book writers and brave thinkers, whose writings and thoughts are like a life form that stimulates, demonstrates and inspires, thus begetting new books and new thoughts by those who come after, as in a continuum.

Authors and publishers who have generously allowed me to quote their words and research.

FOREWORD

The organic gardening movement has been around since the 1920s, mostly in a relatively small way. Those early aims were simple. To respect the soil and to grow fruit, vegetables, herbs and other plants without the use of poisons or disruptive chemical fertilisers. With increasing scientific knowledge and backing, organic growing methods started to take off in a big way from 1970 onwards. It is now a powerful, international movement which is continuing to grow strongly.

We have now reached the inevitable second stage of this important but relatively limited form of environmental consciousness. That's what this remarkable and far-sighted book is all about. *Beyond Organics* is the book that had to be written and Helen Cushing has done a brilliant job. She goes outside the garden, yet still links our gardening activities with the natural environment. Every organic garden, although healthy, different and seemingly quite separate, is still a vital part of a world environment which is clearly deteriorating rapidly. In short, we can't have one without the other and there is no such thing as a garden in isolation.

It is becoming increasingly urgent that we must all do something to help bring the present mindless march towards environmental degradation to a halt — and then reverse it. Most people are worried, but feel helpless. *Beyond Organics* is a powerful call to action. If we can understand our gardens, how they work and how life can be brought back into balance by using organic methods, we can also see the need to extend this ecological balance outside our fences.

The message of this book is quite clear. We can no longer ignore the fact that our gardens are part of a natural world. The spread of organic growing methods has been inspiring. Now let's take the next vital step and start gardening ecologically, too.

Peter Cundall
TASMANIA, 2005

INTRODUCTION

I am not a scientist: I am a gardener and a lover of nature. I am a part of nature, but I can also observe it. My passion for gardening grew out of an urge to be involved with nature, and as I lived in a big city, gardens were the most accessible part of the natural world that I could be actively involved with. I say actively, as opposed to the passive participation in nature that comes from wallowing in the ocean waves, being held by the pageant of sunset, or bushwalking and camping out in wild places.

My obsession with plants, for such it was, started at the age of 16. It was as if a spell had been cast and although the world around me was the same, I saw things I had never seen before. The plant kingdom is vast and into its vastness I leapt. My love affair was with plants more than gardens. Gardens were the vehicle, plants were the essence. Plants in the bush held my fascination as much as garden varieties and I botanised meticulously on bushwalks and absorbed a basic knowledge of ecology as I studied horticulture. Involvement in conservation was part of my family's life before I was born. An understanding that nature mattered was built into my psyche.

As the years of gardening and working in horticulture went by, I participated in and was influenced by trends and developments in the organic movement. I became a gardening writer, and later worked for ABC Television's national gardening program *Gardening Australia*. It was during my time at *Gardening Australia* that the ideas presented in this book took shape. Working in the media, one becomes an observer, exposed to much information and various lines of thought. I had been under the influence of plants for some 25 years. I looked back and saw patterns in the way gardeners responded to the environmental crises which continued to result from the human lifestyle. Organics, I realised, had come a long way since my dabblings in the 1970s when mulch was a new word in the mainstream vocabulary. I saw that over the last three decades gardening and conservation had been drawing closer and closer, but somehow remained separate. I felt they could, and should, become one.

Growing bird-attracting plants and installing frog ponds were responses to habitat crises, just as using plant-derived sprays was a response to the horrors of residual pesticides. But still, there were many subtleties missing from the mix, and I sensed that a paradigm shift needed to happen to take caring gardeners beyond organics and into a deeper ecology of gardening.

This book is the result of those thoughts. It is a personal book; it has stories and observations which are mine alone. It presents both disturbing information about the negative effects many seemingly innocent gardening practices have on the environment and inspiring tales of nature's ways and means of surviving. My aim is to place gardeners and environmentalists on common ground. For after all, we stand together on this Earth, and the fences that divide our gardens do not separate the soil, sun or water that powers each living form.

As housing and development take over more and more land, the importance of gardens in the global ecology also increases. I believe that small is beautiful and that the contribution of each garden to the wider environment should be as rich and positive as we can help it to be. That is all. I hope this book gives an understanding and inspiration which draws people in that direction.

PART I

What is

a garden?

CHAPTER I

A bird's eye view

BEYOND ORGANICS TAKES GARDENING INTO THE REALM of nature conservation in every possible way. For many people, the garden is the main place of interaction with nature, and the only part of the natural environment that they directly influence and look after. And yet, few garden owners have much awareness of the exchanges that constantly occur between their garden and the environment on the other side of the fence. And few garden owners think of their land as being part of the whole landscape that covers planet Earth, inextricably connected and playing, albeit a small one, in the environmental health of this remarkable planet which is home to us all.

The level of environmental awareness in the general community is constantly growing, pushed along by a string of ecological crises that have us worried, even though most of us have comfortable lives filled with opportunity and choice. The natural environment has given us everything we have. Its wealth has become our wealth, and its health is our health. As we shall see in the coming chapters, the last 50 years have been a time of declining health for the natural environment. Many of the symptoms are now acute and the remedies unknown or seem too hard to implement. Few people are in a position to make the decisions that can shift the big picture. But in our gardens we are the decision-makers, the agenda-setters, the policy-brokers. Every big picture is made up of many small jigsaw pieces. Your garden is a jigsaw piece. It contributes to the integrity of the whole masterpiece. It is up to you to paint it well, with knowledge and understanding about how it relates to the rest of the picture in which it is forever embedded.

Going beyond organics means shifting our concept of gardening from one that is based around human needs, desires, aspirations and perceptions, to one that encompasses nature's point of view. It means understanding the big environmental picture that our small gardens are a part of, and gardening in a way that *maximises the garden's positive contribution* to the wellbeing of that wider environment. It means seeing our garden as a piece of the global landscape that interacts constantly with the ecology both within and beyond our fence lines. It means knowing how to manage the garden ecologically, not just organically. In this way, gardening and nature conservation are woven together, smoothly, seamlessly, peacefully.

Many keen organic gardeners do garden in this way. However, it can take years to develop a relationship with the garden that transforms you into an environmental, or ecological, gardener. All the threads that make up organics, plus a few more, must come together to create an approach that allows the ecosystems both within and outside the garden to flourish. You can know a lot about organic gardening techniques and grow a beautiful and bountiful garden of vegetables, fruit and ornamentals without realising that the plants you have chosen have little to offer foraging birds and insects, the style and structure of your garden give no refuge to these same creatures, and perhaps the succulents or bulbs or tree ferns you have bought were harvested from the wild, depleting natural ecosystems that you would want to protect. You may be an expert organic gardener, without being an ecological gardener.

Plus, many people are *not* keen gardeners, but they have a garden and are aware of the environmental crises that face the world. They want to do the right thing in their gardens, but are faced with a bewildering barrage of media and marketing information which is generally 'industry' driven and piecemeal. Most people want their garden to be organic. They understand that garden chemicals harm the environment, and that water has become a limited resource that should be used with care; they know it is good to make compost or feed a worm farm with kitchen and garden 'waste'. More often than not, they find out that gardening in this way is not as easy as the shiny magazine article or TV show made it look, and then blame themselves for doing something wrong. They muddle along, grabbing bits of advice from here and there, planting this and that as it comes along, or finally bringing in a designer to put it all right for them.

There are many demands on people's time. If we are not passionate about something, we tend to settle for second best, and the things that are less valued slip away. This often happens in gardens, as initial waves of inspiration and enthusiasm pass. Environmentally, we can no longer afford to do this. We depend on nature for our survival and quality of life, and although there are many distractions, ultimately when faced with a threat to survival and quality of life, we find that we *are* passionate about those things. Survival is our most basic instinct, and yet, many of our actions are running down the system we depend on for all our needs.

If you have a garden, you have a piece of planet Earth which is your responsibility to manage. With understanding and care, you can maximise its positive interaction with the global environment. That is what is meant by going beyond organics. It is about understanding the environmental implications of what we do or don't do in the garden, and acting on that understanding. In this way the garden comes full circle, as it is re-integrated with the environment out of which it was born. People also generally find that they have a feeling of 'rightness' in gardens that welcome nature.

You may think that your garden is too small to make a difference to the regional or global ecology. Remember that oases exist within the vastness of deserts, and they make a difference, supporting an abundance of life that otherwise would die. So too, your garden can make a difference. Your garden is also connected to other gardens: if your neighbours use environmental gardening principles as well, the total area doubles, triples, quadruples in size, depending on how many neighbours you have.

I have dug up some statistics to back my case that gardens occupy important amounts of ecological space, and throughout the book there are stories and studies which reveal that size, though it does matter, also does not matter. Nature is an opportunist and a risk taker. Puddles teem with life unseen. Each leaf is a microcosm, each mouse a universe.

SMALL IS STILL BEAUTIFUL

We live in a time when the size of the world's natural areas is shrinking. With each passing year, the world's population grows and a larger proportion of that expanding population lives in towns and cities. Australia is already a highly urbanised nation, with 80 percent of people living in urban areas. This is predicted to rise to 88 percent by 2025. Globally, by 2025 it is expected that 60 percent of humanity will be urban dwellers. This trend has ecological implications which are a cause for both concern and creativity. One consequence of this urban explosion is the continued clearing of green space — whether rural or natural — for housing development.

Another is our interest in gardens, and the role they can and do play in local, and therefore global, ecology. Of course, much of the world's urban population does not have gardens at all, particularly in the most crowded nations. However, in the Western world, the popularity of gardening as an activity is on the increase. While the world's natural and pristine environments are decreasing in size, the area occupied by gardens, and the resources being put into them, is growing.

The traditional size of a house block in suburban Australia was once a quarter acre, that is, about 1000 square metres. Even though few modern subdivisions have blocks this size, and people are tending to build larger houses on their smaller blocks, the urban sprawl which characterises Australian cities still contains a significant combined garden area within the city boundaries. Australia's largest city, Sydney, is a good example. It is enormous. In fact, according to the Australian Bureau of Statistics, Greater Sydney covers 12 138 square kilometres; the largest suburban area of any city in the world. This sprawl dwarfs much older cities of much higher populations, such as London and even Beijing. This makes Sydney a geographically and ecologically significant-sized parcel of land. However, before each suburb or subdivision or market garden or orchard (the latter two are being increasingly squeezed) was laid out, these 12 138 square kilometres supported numerous unique ecological communities on several soil types. Its development for housing means that these ecosystems have usually been completely erased.

This seemingly relentless process began less than 250 years ago, and the first population to go was the indigenous human one, which Sydneysiders are inclined to forget, so fleeting was contact between the first Europeans and the Aboriginal peoples of the area. Governor Phillips's forays along what are now Sydney's northern beaches suburbs during the first two years of settlement (1788 and 1789) report the pathos of a dying people, as smallpox devastated the population. By 1790, more than half the Guringai people had died from this disease, their decaying bodies and skeletons littering the sheltered bays that now dance with expensive yachts. With those people went their fine-tuned knowledge of the environment that had nourished them for tens of thousands of years.

Even so, more is known about the flora of Sydney's northern region than about the people who once lived so timelessly amongst its remarkable beauty. The incredible flora of this area, which has a poor soil derived from Hawkesbury sandstone, is one of the most diverse plant communities in the world. Within Australia, it is second only to south-western Western Australia in the number of plant species found. To put this in perspective, south-western Western Australia has perhaps the highest floral diversity of anywhere on planet Earth — around 10 000 species of flowering plants have been identified there. The Cape Floral Kingdom of South Africa, renowned for its botanical richness, has around 8700 species. The flora of northern Sydney is in this league. Fortunately, some reasonably large tracts of it remain intact within national parks and reserves.

The point is: suburbia displaces ecosystems, causing extinctions and vulnerabilities within plant and animal populations. Habitat loss is total when land is cleared, and is compromised by the fragmentation and degradation of remnants of the original ecology which sometimes remain. And yet, within suburbia there *is* open space. It is just divided up by fences and the psychology of human territorialism. In England, where gardening is regarded as a national obsession, nature reserves occupy 85 000 acres, while gardens take up more than 1 million acres. The majority of these gardens are much smaller than Australian gardens, as urban population densities are far greater in England than Australia. As we shall see later in the book, England's habitat crisis has become extreme due to modern agriculture. Wildlife gardening is seen as part of the answer. If you doubt the usefulness of your small garden as a refuge for biodiversity, take heart from these words, extracted from the introduction to, *Creating a Wildlife Garden* by Bob and Liz Gibbons:

> *The proof of this particular pudding has been in the eating — the relatively few people who have pioneered the ideas and the techniques, have shown by their results that such garden mini-habitats can indeed be very rich in species ... there is a vast range of species whose abundance would increase if more gardens were managed in this way.*[1]

When we begin to think of the *combined* size of gardens, rather than the individual size, new possibilities start to emerge in terms of their ecological role. If all the fences were suddenly erased and an aerial photo was taken, the perspective would be vastly different to the one we normally have as we drive or walk in the suburbs: we would have a bird's eye view. And if we care about the Earth, nature's viewpoint is the one we need to cultivate.

EVERY GARDEN CAN AND DOES PROVIDE HABITAT FOR a range of indigenous and non-indigenous species, including those that come and go, like birds, butterflies and other insects, frogs, lizards and small mammals. Also included in the list of comers and goers could be the so-called 'garden escapes', that is, the garden plants that ignore the boundary fences, venturing happily into the wide

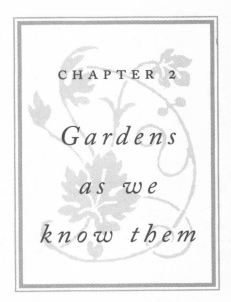

CHAPTER 2

Gardens

as we

know them

world where they are eventually labelled 'weeds'. As understanding and awareness of the need to be involved in maintaining regional biodiversity grows, the relevance of gardens in this task has become apparent.

The problem of declining natural green space and the attendant drop in biodiversity is only one reason, albeit a major one, for moving beyond organics and into environmental gardening. However, gardeners also need to understand the direct negative environmental consequences of some gardening practices: discontinuing these practices is vital to ecologically responsible gardening. I am not just talking here about harmful chemicals, which most of us have stopped using by now. There are many subtler gardening habits which are ecologically detrimental and yet are acceptable within organics. The way we garden and its environmental implications are explored in greater depth in *Part 2 — The way we garden*.

The starting point for gardening in this way is understanding that a garden is a set of ecosystems in itself and that the garden is not an island. As we have said, it interacts with the wider environment. It is easy to see that the internal ecology of any garden is constantly affected by the gardener/owner, whether that person is conscious of the garden in this way or not. But we tend to think less about the ongoing interaction with the ecology *beyond* the fence. It can be positive or negative, and is likely to be a bit of both. Environmental gardening recognises these realities. Knowing that the small patches of land we call gardens can be biologically important at a time when many global ecosystems are in crisis, the gardener develops the garden in a way that both satisfies the human needs of functionality and aesthetics while maximising the benefits to the ecology of the region.

It is also important to acknowledge and be influenced by the recognition that originally an independent, 'wild' ecology existed on the piece of land, without direct human input. This may have been 5000 years ago, or five years ago. By seeing our land with this in mind, instead of merely as a place for us to use while we live there, our viewpoint starts to shift and broaden. We are hearing more and more about the global biodiversity crisis as an increasing number of wild species becomes endangered or extinct and the food-crop gene pool shrinks under the weight of agribusiness. However, most of the time we forget that our own backyards were once homes and feeding grounds for all sorts of species, from both the plant and animal kingdoms. For some of the species that are now in trouble, as well as for others who are not yet in dire straits, it is possible to make our gardens into havens once more.

THE GARDEN IS A HAVEN

For indeed, gardens have been havens and refuges since the earliest of civilisations. These early gardens were walled, giving refuge and protection to the gardens themselves, as well as the people in them. We are not talking about gardens set in the sprawling suburbs of cities with CBDs that scrape the sky and grids of black roads forming boundary after boundary, obscuring soft landscape and linking human with human. The first gardens of the early civilisations formed edges to the uncivilised. It is hard for us to imagine what that really meant. In those days, the world was raw. There were wild animals and wild people. The buffer between life and death was faint. Protection was mainly up to the individual. Those with private gardens had wealth and therefore the chance of leisure and softness in a tough world of survival. Within the walls of a garden a refuge could be made, relaxation was possible, for people and plants alike. The gentleness of water and greenery, of control and design, separated the people and their plants from the lawlessness beyond the wall.

The earliest records of garden layouts are found in the tombs of the Egyptians. The oldest is a wooden model of a walled garden dating from around 2000 BCE. Painted green, it shows a house and a fish pond shaded by trees. From about 1085 BCE, tomb paintings began to show simple garden layouts. Interestingly, these early walled gardens, enclosing a formal rectangular pool surrounded by flowerbeds and shade trees, have a classical elegance in their structure which garden designers throughout history have emulated. The beauty and peace that made these first gardens into havens from the untamed outside remain enduring qualities in the meaning of gardens to the human psyche.

Gardens are still places of refuge, havens for both plants and their people. The wildness we need refuge from today, however, is mostly of our own making. The garden's edge takes us from the public to the private; from the fast-paced life into a realm where, if we want to, we can simply watch the grass grow; from the industrial to the natural; and hopefully, from the stressful to the restful.

However, gardens are also a refuge of a different type. Think beyond the people in the modern complex of town and city living. In amongst all that bitumen and cement there are still some birds and bats and lizards and frogs and bees and other winged and creeping things that need homes and havens. Remember also the plants that used to grow where buildings and factories have sprouted in all their solid, barren rigidity. I mean the original plants, the ones that nature chose, planted by no hand and not tilled or kept by anyone. Before development (whether urban or rural), each ecosystem in each and every part of the world was home to many species. Even in the densest cities, some of those species have survived, finding homes where they may. Gardens are now refuges for these organisms as well — havens for wild things — because their original ecosystems have gone.

The choices of garden style and plantings that we make are usually influenced by fashion, expression, practicality, house style. What would happen to our gardens if we also considered those other life forms in our designs? We could think about what *they* need, in the desert of our making, the landscape of suburban sprawl and industrial hardness. Think of the refuge that a garden can be to the bits of wild nature that remain in the places people now dominate. Nowadays, those bits of wild nature are referred to as centres of 'biodiversity' and there is more and more information about the importance of maintaining this biodiversity, as the list of species extinctions worldwide accelerates at an alarming pace.

Perhaps as much as the garden owners of times past needed to keep the wild things out, we now need to think about letting them in, if for no other reason than they have nowhere else to live. Our gardens can be oases in the built deserts that stretch wider and wider. This approach to gardening is known variously as 'habitat gardening', 'wildlife gardening' and 'flora for fauna' gardening. It is increasingly becoming a component of the organic garden, although it is not really about organics. It is broader; it is about the environment. It is a subject that we will return to in considerable depth, as we develop an understanding of the garden ecosystem and the dynamism of its relationship to the world over the boundary fence.

THE GARDEN IS FOR EATING

Food production has been a key role of gardens since the domestication of plants began thousands of years ago. The relationship between gardeners and food crops is a unique one, and as we shall see, the food garden has been a remarkable cradle of biodiversity in itself.

Food gardens, rather than large-scale agriculture, traditionally provided communities with a high percentage of their diet. This was done very successfully and sustainably in many places. In his classic book, *An Agricultural Testament*, Sir Albert Howard — regarded as the 'father of organics' — singles out the small size of farms in China and India as a key to their success in maintaining productivity for thousands of years. He writes, 'The agricultural practices of the Orient have passed the supreme test — they are almost as permanent as those of the primeval forest, of the prairie or of the ocean. The small holdings of China, for example, are still maintaining a steady output and there is no loss of fertility after 40 centuries of management.[1]

Asking himself what are the characteristics of these farms, Howard states firstly and most emphatically that 'the holdings are minute'. They were (and may still be) managed as intensively as a garden, and were completely organic in the modern sense of the word. It was a case of small is beautiful, and it was the close relationship between peasant farmers and their farms and gardens all over the world that created the vast and life-sustaining diversity of food crops which has been eroded in so short a time by modern agricultural science.

Food gardening has a vital role to play in the maintenance of global biodiversity, as well as the cultural diversity of the human race. It is from the food gardens that the world's wondrous collage of flavours has been brought forth to inspire the ingenuity and creativity of generations of chefs going about their duties with their cooking pots. It is in the food garden that people have experienced and participated in an interdependence with plants that is unique. The people need the plants of these gardens, but also, the plants need the people. Plant selection and seed-saving across the centuries and millennia have resulted in thousands of domesticated food-crop varieties. These strains have been selected not only for flavour but also for their adaptations to local conditions. It is in this heritage that the genes for resistance to many adversities have been cultivated. For example, tolerance to drought, frost and wind, resistance to pests and diseases, adaptation to soil types, to short seasons, to long seasons, to hot sun, to low light and on it goes. It is to this heritage that modern plant breeders turn for the wonder genes they crave. But it is a resource dependent on the lifestyle of a peasant culture that is no longer valued. And that which is not valued, is lost. The remnants of this genetic treasure trove increasingly depend on seedbanks for survival, although there is certainly quite an active grassroots movement working to keep the dynamic connection between the food-crop gene pool and people.

The expression of culture in food gardening is not only seen in cuisine and plant selection. It takes many forms in gardens themselves, from the extreme ornamental to the simple, semi-wild gardens of women in the Amazon jungle. Here's what I mean.

At the extreme end of design, the French, those masters of garden formality and plant sculpting, developed, perhaps inevitably, the kitchen garden into high art, bringing the fussy, geometric parterre into the domain of the potager. Meticulously designed and laid out, vegetables and herbs are arranged in plantings based on shape, form, colour and texture. Perfectly espaliered fruit trees adorn the garden wall, perhaps fan-shaped, perhaps angular, both beautiful and abundant. Typically, the French love of fine food is not compromised in the visual aesthetics of these not-a-hair-out-of-place vegie patches. Fruit and vegetable varieties in France are grown specifically for particular cooking styles, flavours and recipes, as well as for their good looks. It should be mentioned, however, that French kitchen gardens also include rambling, half-wild creations spilling with charm and mystery. These are at the romantic end of the potager tradition. The common ground, so to speak, is in the blending of flowers and food plants. The potager always includes flowers, to bring the bees and other insects and birds that are needed to keep the garden ecology in balance.

Traditionally, therefore, they are also environmental gardens.

At the other end of the design spectrum are the gardens of the Kayapo Indians, deep in the Brazilian Amazon. The Kayapo women keep the gardens. Their helpers are millions of tiny red ants. The women plant mixed plots of vegetables including maize, climbing beans, squash and cassava. In the lush jungle climate, the vigorous bean vines quickly become a rampant tangle with the potential to smother the young cassava plants. Enter the little red ant, a benign creature of the Kayapo fields. As the beans gain a stranglehold, and the strong maize stalks push skyward, the vulnerable cassava secretes a sweet nectar, irresistible to the ants. Hordes of them appear, making paths through the garden to reach the coveted nectar. To facilitate their single-minded feeding frenzy, the ants make paths and clear the invading bean vines from the cassava plants. The bean plants are not destroyed by the ants; they are merely pruned and redirected to grow up the maize stalks. Is it any wonder that the women revere these tiny garden helpers? Imagine the time and sweat it would take to perform this task by hand.

Each year there is a maize festival at which the Kayapo women show their reverence for the processes of nature by decorating their faces with a paste coloured crimson by the crushed bodies of the ants. The integration of nature with Kayapo culture is expressed in this friendship, such as it is, between the women, the red ants and the gardens.

Most food-gardening styles fall between the high art of the French parterre and the relaxed co-existence of the red ants and the Kayapo women. Scenes of practical productivity in which the owners of bent backs and wide-brimmed hats dig and push barrows in the sweet light of spring are somehow a warm and comforting sight. A garden with rows of sweet corn growing tall, green and lush against a blue-drenched summer sky; spectacular clouds of cumulus cauliflower bubbling out of strong, green cradles of leafiness; cheeky sparrows perched on a scarecrow's broken hat; stacks of tomato stakes awaiting their season of usefulness; grapevines scrambling over trellises; lemon trees bulging with great yellow droplets of fruit as bees bumble and buzz in heaven-scented blossom; potted herbs balanced on window sills; the gardener working patiently — such images seem to contain the very essence of gardening.

The environmental garden doesn't *need* to include food growing, but it can. I would say, however, that the environmental garden of today should not be *only* a food garden. Affluence brings choice, and in the West there are few people who need to put all their garden space under food to survive. The environmental gardener considers the food needs of other species as well as humans, and designs and plants accordingly.

It should be acknowledged here that it is food gardeners who have led the development of the organic-gardening movement in the last 30–40 years. The reason for this may be the impossible-to-avoid and unpalatable connection between applying poison to food and then harvesting and sharing that food with your loved ones. I'm sure that is a strongly motivating factor, however, I think there is more to it than that.

In an age when an abundance of good-looking, polished and packaged fruit and vegetables is easily and cheaply bought, it takes passion and dedication to put in the time and effort to grow your own. It requires hard, constant work to maintain a truly productive food garden. And doing it organically doesn't make the job any easier, especially in Australia where soils are relatively low in organic matter and nutrient, and the climate is often one of drying winds, baking suns or flooding rains.

The desire to grow food for one's family, when it would be so much easier not to, expresses a direct connection with nature in a way that other forms of gardening or other types of nature contact do not. There is an aspect of care and responsibility implicit in the idea of growing your own food when it is by choice. People with those qualities are likely to feel the same sentiments of care and responsibility towards the soil they till, the birds whose song drifts out of trees, and the bees, dragonflies and butterflies whose wings beat gently through the blankness of air. A reverence for nature, akin to that of the Kayapo women, exists in the hearts and minds of organic gardeners. This spark of connection is an important one, which motivates the move beyond organics and towards the idea of gardening from nature's point of view.

THE GARDEN IS FOR BEAUTY

While the environmental garden aims to feed the birds and the bees and maybe the people, for many gardeners the source of inspiration is an aesthetic one. They want to create and be surrounded by beauty. They desire a style of garden which compliments their house. They have a sense of ownership which involves using the space known as a garden for its visual and emotional appeal to themselves. For many, the existence of a garden and the choice of plants does not need any practical justification. As a creative art, gardening uses the bounty of nature like no other form of human expression. While the words of poets, the arrangements of musicians and the brush strokes of painters evoke and interpret nature's spirit and moods, the garden designer works with the multidimensional landscape, the changes and inconsistencies of season, and the shifting needs and appearance of life forms.

Gertrude Jekyll remains one of England's most inspired — and inspiring — garden artists. In her book, *Wood and Garden*, she wrote, 'For planting ground is painting a landscape with living things and I hold that good gardening takes rank within the bounds of the fine arts, so I hold that to plant well needs an artist of no mean capacity'.[2] A prolific writer as well as gardener and designer, Jekyll's description of colour use in the herbaceous border is an insight into the attention to detail, the depth of understanding and the care that is needed to create great art with plants:

The planting of the border is designed to show a distinct scheme of colour arrangement ... Looked at from a little way forward, for a wide space of grass allows this point of view, the whole border can be seen as one picture, the cool colouring at the ends enhancing the brilliant warmth of the middle. Then, passing along the wide path next to the border the value of colour-arrangement is still more strongly felt. Each portion now becomes a picture in itself, and every one is of such a colouring that it best prepares the eye, in accordance with natural law, for what is to follow. Standing for a few moments before the endmost region of grey and blue, and saturating the eye to its utmost capacity with these colours, it passes with extraordinary avidity to the succeeding yellows. These intermingle in a pleasant harmony with the reds and scarlets, blood-reds and clarets, and then lead again to yellows. Now the eye has again become saturated, this time with the rich colouring, and has therefore, by the law of complementary colour, acquired a strong appetite for the greys and purples. These therefore assume an appearance of brilliancy that they would not have had without the preparation provided by their recently received complementary colour.[3]

The genius of Gertrude Jekyll brought the art of colour gardening to a pinnacle. Such design brilliance leaves a legacy of theory and example which inspires and instructs those who come after. The role of beauty in gardens is vital. It is the key motivator for many garden owners, although few bring their vision to reality. Nevertheless, along the way these gardeners develop a relationship with the plants they nurture and with the nature they work with. These relationships often take over from the original ideal of creating a picture-perfect garden. Relationships are like that. Once you start caring for a small plant, perhaps grown with your own hand from a seed or cutting, you go through the ups and downs of life with it, because it is alive. While the original motivation was to create the vision held in the mind's eye, or seen on the pages of the magazine or book, most gardeners find that they are extremely forgiving and tolerant when the rose or camellia of which they had such high expectations doesn't reach full potential. Each flower produced is a triumph, treasured like the paintings of a child. The little prince of the book by that name gave his heart and soul and ultimately his body in his devotional quest to care for the vain, demanding rose that grew so enigmatically on his lonely asteroid. Touched originally by beauty, many gardeners, like the prince, make friends with their plants and forgive their failings. The achievement of the big picture often loses its importance as the focus shifts to the individuals within the picture. This relationship is important, as it is the beginning of caring for more than appearance, and with it comes a need and an urge to understand what is going on in the nature of the garden.

Beauty in the garden is important — at the micro level of individual plants and at the macro level of the whole garden as a picture. Gardens are part of our culture as much as part of the human habitat. It's important that our relationship with them is dynamic and sympathetic. There are many layers to beauty, and as awareness of the garden as part of nature develops, its multidimensional, or layered, beauty becomes apparent. There are many beauties that do not show up in the colourful photographs that advertise flowers. Such as the parts of the garden that are dark and unseen, moving with worms and grubs and water, the messy corners where lizards and beetles and fungi hide, and that prickly, overgrown, 'unattractive' shrubbery against the back fence in the heart of which tiny nestlings grow safe, well-fed and unknown.

THE GARDEN IS SACRED

Far away from the flower borders of England another landscape form of delicate and serene beauty evolved in Japan, a country renowned for the distinctive and precise art of its gardens. In the highly aesthetic layout of Japanese gardens the relationship to nature, and so to spirit, is a key element. To Western eyes, Japanese gardens are deeply stylised, controlled and symbolic. But what do the Japanese see in their gardens?

Josiah Conder's classic, *Landscape Gardening in Japan*, was first published in 1893. His opening paragraph takes us straight to the heart of garden-meaning in Japan:

A garden in Japan is a representation of the scenery of the country ... Favourite rural spots and famous views serve as models for its composition and arrangement. The laws of natural growth and distribution are closely studied and punctiliously applied in the management of even the smallest detail. The artificial hills, rocks, lakes, torrent beds and cascades of gardens are copied from striking features in the varied landscape of the country.[4]

Interestingly, Conder also says, 'Japanese writers point to India as the original source from whence ideas of garden composition were derived.' He continues, 'But the influence which India has exercised upon the gardening art as practised in this country has been one of religion and sentiment rather than of method and arrangement.'[5]

I have never been to Japan. But in the remote alpine landscapes of Tasmania I have seen places that could pass as Japanese gardens. The stunted forms of ancient conifers bonsaied by snow and wind and deep cold grow bravely and elegantly against lichen-painted boulders on the edges of lakes and tarns dark and perfect with reflection. Tiny islands in the lakes repeat the motif of bonsai and boulder and moss. Streams of purist water run over rounded rocks, spilling out of and into the lakes, their sound travelling through the sharp, clear air in that mesmerising way of flowing water. If this is also how the snows and waters and winters of Japan carve its landscape, then the gardens are indeed remarkable representations of nature at its most poignant, rather than the highly stylised designs we usually perceive.

There is a very direct connection between wild nature and people in

Japanese gardens. Meaning derived from religious philosophy becomes the bridge linking human expression with nature. This occurs in a more explicit way in cultures where certain plants are grown because of religious and symbolic associations, as in classical Greece and ancient and modern India. Cypress trees, representing mortality and eternity, were planted in groves around the temples of ancient Greece and Mesopotamia. Many trees were dedicated to the gods — oaks were associated with Zeus, olives with Athena and poplars with Hercules.

In India, the natural and the sacred are still linked through plantings that represent deities and the qualities they embody. I recall the tall, slender form of a glossy-leaved tree grown in the ashrams (spiritual communities) I visited, where they bordered the lawns and lined the roads. When I enquired what the tree was, I was told simply 'It is the ashoka tree, it is sacred.' Further research revealed that *ashoka* is a Sanskrit word meaning 'without grief'. Another name for the same tree in a different Indian language means 'the tree of love blossoms'. Dedicated to the Hindu god of love, Kama Deva, the ashoka (*Saraca indica*) is said to heal deep sorrow and bring inner harmony and joy.

Another plant I often saw growing in shrines, both in domestic gardens and in ashrams, was the delicate-looking *tulsi*. I recognised it as sacred basil. This time I was told it brings long life and good health. Dedicated to the great god Vishnu, the preserver, its woody stem is used to make beads for malas, the rosary used in yogic meditation.

A profound sense of the sacred infuses such plantings. However, without an understanding of the meaning behind these plantings, the Western eye and mind perceive only the plants themselves, or in Japan, the extreme aesthetics of the Zen garden. Nevertheless, the sense of stillness and harmony which come from the design are 'felt', even with-out direct understanding or knowledge of the 'religion and sentiment' behind the 'method and arrangement'. A reverence for and connection with nature is inherent and intended in these gardens and plantings.

Interestingly, devoted gardeners also often describe their experience or relationship with the garden as *spiritual*. Gardens are valued as places for reflection and for peace, places where we can be refreshed and nourished by nature. These are needs of the human spirit, and again and again, we turn to gardens to fulfil these needs. Very often it is naturalistic gardens that we are most readily soothed by, an approach to garden design which takes us one step closer to the idea of environ-mental gardening.

THE GARDEN MERGES WITH NATURE

In any discussion of the reproduction of nature by garden designers, England's 18th-century genius 'Capability' Brown has to be men-tioned. When the English tide began to turn against the influence of French formality, a move towards the natural and irregular gathered momentum. Brown was the most important of the designers responsible for the transformation of English estates into 'parks' on a grand scale. He ruthlessly removed the straight lines and avenues planted under French influence. A master of the grand vision, he shaped and planted landscapes which would take a hundred or more years to mature. With incredible energy, he widened rivers, made lakes, moved earth into gentle undulations, planted groves and clumps and belts made up of hundreds of thousands of trees, both native and exotic. Capability Brown perfected what we now think of as the classical English landscape. He worked with passion and extraordinary expertise as he sought to create scenes which would be perfect not only for the owner, but also for poets and painters. Brown's attention to detail was meticulous from the planning through to the completion of construction and planting.

The scale of Brown's work is rare, but his vision of creating naturalistic landscapes is shared by many gardeners and designers. Here, in Australia, the most beloved of our landscape designers from the 20th century seem to have worked at evolving gardens that reflect the natural landscape. Edna Walling is possibly the most renowned.

Strongly influenced by Gertrude Jekyll, Walling followed this powerful woman's footsteps in more than just design style. Like Jekyll, she gardened as well as designed, and Walling was also a talented amateur photographer and an inspired garden writer. Edna's projects also extended into house and village design. All was to be integrated. The cottages she designed were part and parcel of the garden landscape, and the outlooks from the cottage windows must be pictures uncontrived, restful and seamless. Her ideas of linking house and garden are fashionable in today's lifestyle and leisure-oriented culture. On this topic in *A Gardener's Log* she wrote:

> It is really rather amazing that we have copies of the English style rather than Spanish and Italian, because in this climate protection from hot winds is essential to civilised living. Here in Australia quite intelligent people continue to live in houses that get hot enough to roast them, and remarkably few have pergola-covered living rooms outside. The majority have only two doors, so that to enter the garden you must go to the back door or the front

door. Not to be able to bring the garden into the living room on a summer day would be intolerable to me. To be able to walk out onto cool paving that has just been hosed down, and to spread a cloth on a long, low table under vines for a late evening meal, is not a luxury, it is essential.[6]

Originally from England, Walling developed a love for Australian plants and the landscape they grew in. She championed the use of native plants in gardens and was a vocal and articulate conservationist, humble in her declaration that nature's arrangements achieved a grace and elegance which needed no improvement. She wrote:

How very necessary it is to train ourselves to observe the natural beauty around us so that in the exuberance of our beautification schemes we shall not do things that disturb and eventually destroy the landscape ... seldom, if ever, do we achieve the quiet perfection of nature's planting. The roadways around Mooroolbark are particularly lovely; there are endless and most varied pictures for miles. One road is most picturesque with its fringe of paperbarks clustered along the boundary fences ... The closely clustered trunks and the quaint tufts of dark-green foliage etched against the evening sky, with the unbroken foreground of native grass, made one devoutly hope that this picture would never be destroyed by any other planting.[7]

This identification with the landscape continues to be developed by thoughtful and reflective designers, as modern Australian culture subtly lets go of its European underpinnings, and deepens its connection with the soil its people walk upon and its plants grow in. Renowned designer Gordon Ford writes in his book, *Gordon Ford: The Natural Australian Garden*: 'We must feel part of the land we walk on and love the plants that grow there ... if we are to achieve a spirit in a garden.'[8] Lacking an ancient tradition of sacred plants and plantings, the relationship of gardens to the spiritual dimension finds more general expression through a relationship with nature. As Ford puts it, 'I believe that gardens offer us something beyond the material world. They provide a spiritual component allowing us to participate in the wonder and mystery of creation.'[9]

Importantly for the environment in Australia, this feeling, that there is a dimension to gardening which relates to something deeper in the human spirit, has led to design that connects the garden back to nature. Ellis Stones was another important innovator in the development of an Australian gardening aesthetic based around the forms and plants of the natural landscape. A survivor of Gallipoli, Stones built many of the stone walls, ponds and rock features which are so important to the naturalistic quality of Edna Walling's gardens. He moved from a focus on construction to design, always seeking to bring environmental values into the city gardens he created. In the foreword to Ford's book, Graeme Law writes of Gordon Ford and Ellis Stones, 'Their gardens reflected a regional ecology ... another expression of acceptance of our identity and place.'[10]

Contemporary and award-winning landscape consultant Paul Thompson creates gardens largely based on plant species native to the region where the garden is located. He takes great care with plant selection, spending much time researching a wide variety of plants which are often difficult to source, but result in the growing of a garden that belongs to its locale. No aesthetic compromise is made by taking this approach, rather, his attention to detail and sensitivity to the greater landscape in which the garden exists brings about gardens of remarkable subtlety, depth and beauty. The birds and other creatures that find refuge in such gardens are part of their dynamic, part of the owner's experience of the garden. He writes in the introduction to *Australian Planting Design*, 'Australian gardens are not icons of status, they are at their best when they are personal expressions of a nurturing philosophy ... Australians are beginning to develop an urban landscape that belongs to the land and its history.'[11]

Designers with this inclination towards nature are searching for and finding a new depth in their approach to gardens. Through their openness they are developing the connection between people and nature that is intrinsic to sensitive gardening. Their approach is shot-through with care for *life*. They work from the premise that beauty is more than skin deep, that it has expression and value beyond the eyes of the beholder and that nature's forms and structures bring a depth and spirit to gardens that is important.

There is acknowledgement in this approach of the fact that gardens are alive — they are a living, breathing, fading, dying, dynamic collection of interacting organisms and non-living things. Science calls this an ecosystem. An essential organism in the matrix of the garden ecosystem is the human being, who determines much of its make-up.

We human beings have many different perceptions of, purposes for, and approaches to the whole idea of having a garden. Several themes run through the history of gardening over time and across cultures, based on the values, desires, inspirations and needs of the gardeners. They are expressions of the human mind in its interaction with nature. They arise from human perspectives to do with spirituality, food production, art and the urge to re-create nature.

At a time when our global ecology is under extraordinary strain from human impact, the purpose of this book is to present another perspective on gardening. That is, to look at the garden from nature's point of view, from the big picture right down to the minutiae, shifting our paradigm of what a garden is so that we see the garden as part of the global ecology, rather than merely a plot of land within our boundary fence.

People have been gardening for thousands of years, in ways that were appropriate to their times, as environmental gardening is now appropriate to our times. Taking a brief look at some key aspects of the meaning of gardens through history helps us to understand their place deep in the human psyche and understand how we have arrived at the most commonly held gardening paradigm — that gardens are our territory within which we express ourselves according to the functions and aesthetics we desire.

Understanding where we have come from usually makes it easier to move on — in this case, to shift the garden paradigm from one based around people to one that is based around the ecological role of a garden. In his book, *The Nature of Gardens*, Peter Timms describes the process of change in relation to leaving a garden that was an important part of his life: 'Crucially, this garden has amply fulfilled its main purpose, and, hopefully, will go on doing so: it is a catalyst for experience, for the gaining of knowledge and understanding. It is, in a word, transformative … For in the end, growth depends upon our ability to disown what we have inherited.'[12]

Before taking a closer look at what we have inherited, in *Part 2 — The way we garden*, think for a moment about the garden's perception of itself. This is a way of looking that takes us beyond the limitations of culture and conditioning which colour our approach to gardens. The reason for doing this is because many gardeners care very much about the environment, but have little understanding of the ecosystems within their gardens and of the interactions of their garden with the world beyond the fence line.

What, then, is a garden when perceived as environment?

STRANGELY, AND PERHAPS SADLY, IT WAS RACHEL Carson's exposé of the sinister effects of the virtually indiscriminate use of modern insecticides in *Silent Spring* (1962) that so graphically illustrated the subtle and intricate linkage of life to life that creates the global ecology, and warned of the implications of ignoring this reality. This information, though initially controversial,

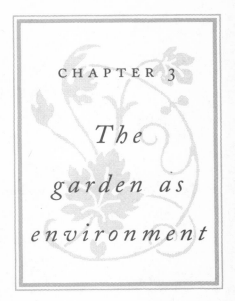

CHAPTER 3

The garden as environment

spearheaded the environmental movement as we know it in a culture whose alienation from nature had allowed it to view nature and people as separate. It is more than 40 years since *Silent Spring* was published. Slowly, slowly, the waves and ripples that spread out from the bombshell of Carson's exposé have crept further and further, seeping into the sands of the collective consciousness and conscience. These ripples have washed through our gardens, and continue to do so. Organic gardening has finally become mainstream, the basis of an industry in itself, but more on this later, when we look into the evolution of organic gardening in *Part 3 — The evolution of modern gardening*. For now, a walk into the ecology of a garden.

FENCES ARE AN ILLUSION

The lawn runs along the fence line, cool and damp and soft, a blend of grasses, clover, daisies and flat weeds, bespeaking spongy soil below. An ant crawls through the sharp, green blades, labouring with a wattle seed from the neighbour's bush. A startled grasshopper leaps. A bee buzzes in the clover, stealing nectar and bringing pollen from flowers across the road. A breeze drifts across the landscape, carrying the scent of jasmine from somewhere. It brings to mind China, India, cups of fragrant tea. The sun is warm. A fly buzzes and settles, buzzes and settles, bringing to mind dung, germs, maggots. A cloud obscures the sun, and the brightness is gone. A kookaburra laughs in the distance, perhaps it has just downed a snake. Below ground there is fertile, strong soil, teeming with life, activity everywhere. Threadlike root hairs push through the soil, under the fence, following worm tunnels and making their own passageways past nesting ants, pupating beetles, pressing on, mindlessly unaware of the blind white grubs that single-mindedly chew on roots. A cicada prepares to emerge after a 17-year metamorphosis. There is a cricket, quiet in the dark. Earthworms patiently burrow, spiders nestle in holes. Wasps hunt for the grubs that hunt for the roots that absorb nutrients. Water seeps downhill. This is a *simple* snapshot of the cool underworld.

Above ground, in the bright Australian light, a gum tree grows by the fence, an endless line of ants marching up its trunk. Scribbles in the bark tell of scribbling insects. Keen eyes might spot a deftly camouflaged moth, close against the pale brown bark. Gum oozes from an upper limb, blocking the hole of a soft-bodied borer. A flock of cockatoos land squawking in the upper branches, where a stick insect invisibly chews on leaves. The leaves are black-dotted with gum-tree scale and glisten with the honeydew of lerps. Gaudy cup moth caterpillars, looking like Chinese junks, also chew on the leaves. Fat cicadas are heard but not seen, their magnificent loudness inhabiting the summer's heat, their cast-off shells clinging to the bark like memories. Some fluffy froth gives away the presence of a spittle bug. It is an old tree. The fruiting bodies of wood-rot fungi emerge like dinner plates from the solid-looking trunk. Its knobbly roots push at the fence palings. Under the bark is the webbing of spiders, the crawling of beetles, the holes of borers and shy tree crickets, the threading mycelium of fungi like a net that holds all together, but actually is pulling all apart. Up high is a hollow, where a sleeping possum is curled with its baby. The scent of eucalyptus oil and the too-sweet nectar of gum blossom are on the hot air. The blossom vibrates with bees filling their honey baskets, as iridescent jewel beetles silently sip nectar.

Downhill from the gum tree is a glade where the geometric leaves of a gentle, spreading Japanese maple filter the sunlight over a pond. A mosaic of glowing moss and scraps of lichen decorate rocks, the water ripples as a breeze brings fallen leaves and spent blossom petals into the pond. Stillness returns, and with it a pair of dragonflies. Their compound eyes have thousands of lenses each; they can look up and down at the same time. Their two sets of wings beat 20–30 times per second, moving simultaneously in different directions. They can fly at up to 88.5 km/h and eat as many as 600 insects each day. The dappled light plays with those filigree wings, as it has done with wings of this type for more than 200 million years. Water irises rise skyward, strong stalks, coquettish flowers; waterlilies lounge on the surface; tadpoles squirm and squiggle amongst the leaves and weeds. The cool of the water moves through the air. Frogs croak, fish jump, a bird splashes its careful wings as it bathes. Down below in the bottom mud there is decay, and strange, wordless critters hide. In the cool cracks between rocks, ferns uncurl. There is a whole society of birds, insects, reptiles, mammals who come here to drink, wash and feed, each attracted by the water, and also by each other, with some becoming the meals of others. Plus there are the unseen millions, billions, of micro-organisms — the politics of ecology requires that this silent majority are not forgotten.

These universes of activity are ecosystems, the ecology of our gardens. Their strange and interesting and eccentric inhabitants are closer than our next-door neighbours. We share our gardens with them.

The story repeats throughout the garden. In the mulch layers, in the compost heap, in fruit trees, vegetable beds, flower gardens, shrubberies, ponds, puddles, piles of rocks and neglected garden sheds. Put them all together, and the result is the garden ecosystem. It is a complex community, like a forest or grassland or coastal ecosystem, threaded through with interconnections and relationships, and interacting with the world and the environment beyond its boundaries. Through this world walks the gardener, adjusting this and that, according to his or her knowledge and whim.

The skilled gardener is a manipulator, working the system for his or her own ends. Like nature, the gardener works with epicentres and so fosters ecosystems, although this is not usually the intention. What do I mean by epicentres? Think of the gum tree and the pond described above. These are epicentres, each a base structure around which a whole complexity of life develops. Here is another example.

A rock that has been heated by the sun holds that heat for a while, releasing it after sundown. Life forms find that warmer place and take up residence, their nature depending also on the availability of water, which flows through these ecosystems according to the invisible law of gravity. The seemingly lifeless rock spawns biodiversity. A brick or stone wall facing the sun in a garden does the same thing, and so gardeners plant heat-loving and frost-tender species beneath that wall, perhaps an orange tree, and make sure there is water. Uninvited, independent life forms will also arrive — weeds that love light and shelter and some dampness to make life easy; aphids on the new citrus growth, then the birds and ladybirds that feed on them; lizards, for the warmth and also to feed on the tiny insects; spiders to weave and catch; ants to 'farm' scale on glossy, fussed-over citrus branches; sooty moulds to live on the honey dew produced by the scale and fed on by the ants … This whole society revolves around the architecture of a wall and some plants: the epicentre around which it all moves. A city paved in bitumen and built of concrete and brick stays warmer at night than the same landscape covered in grass. Bodies of water also store and release heat, modifying the climate around them to an extent determined by their size. These heat banks create microclimates which in turn create a mini-ecosystem, as life, ever the opportunist, responds to difference.

Within these ecologies the cycles of nature occur. The carbon cycle, the nitrogen cycle, the water cycle; plus cycles of oxygen, phosphorous, sulphur, and many more. In a garden system, the gardener manipulates some of these for his or her own purposes. For example, in fertilising and watering. This is where some problems can emerge, as the gardener's understanding may be quite clinical and narrow, based on achieving a single gardening goal, without due consideration of the complex interactions that can proceed from the action. For example, a nutrient deficiency in a plant is diagnosed. A fertiliser is purchased in a bag or box or bottle. A measurement is made. The stuff is 'applied'. The plant (hopefully) loses the deficiency symptoms. But the gardener's awareness is limited to the appearance of the plant. There is little, if any, thought for the cycling of that nutrient in the system.

Where did the nutrient come from, and where else will it go?

Water is another cycle that gardeners and farmers very actively influence without due thought for the big picture. A plant wilts. Water stress is diagnosed. Water is applied. The plant recovers. But the water didn't start or stop with our application of it.

Where has the water come from and where else will it go?

Obviously, the same principle applies to the application of poisons, but there is more awareness of the potential impact of poisons than of fertiliser and water, which seem relatively benign. Especially if the fertiliser is organic. Much has been written about the persistence and movement of pesticides in the environment, so I won't repeat that information here. The point is that this divorcing of our actions from the movement of materials in the system can have catastrophic results that reach far beyond our garden gates. I am thinking of algal blooms that are encouraged both by the seeping of excess nitrogen and phosphorous into water systems, and by the slow flows in rivers that are increasingly common due to damming and large volumes of water being taken for irrigation. The nutrients come from various sources, including sewerage, detergents and fertiliser. The fertiliser we apply, whether natural or synthesised, must be water-soluble for uptake by plants. It merges into the water we apply (or that comes from rain), and together they continue their endless journey, travelling out of our garden or farm and into a river system, along with countless other applications of nitrogen, phosphorous and water to all those other gardens and farms that have fences and boundaries. Or think they do.

The boundaries exist only in the minds of the property owners, where they allow that owner to limit his or her sense of responsibility to the space within those fences. It is easy to think that we don't have much impact, because our land or garden is not so big. But the biosphere is fenceless, and time is long, longer than the river. The effect on the environment beyond our fence is the combined effect of many individuals, over many years, many generations. In the same way, our concept of ecosystems is generally flawed, because it packages them into neat concepts that satisfy our desire to contain and present our understanding, as though ecosystems also have fences. But they don't.

I am also thinking of the salination of vast areas of agricultural land and even of suburban gardens that happens when we take water from here and apply it to there without due consideration of the chemical interactions and reactions that are part of the cycling, the continuous cycling, that occurs in nature. First we remove the vegetation. The trees with their deep roots and their vital role in the water cycle are cut down to make way for farms or houses. Then we plant shallow-rooted crops and irrigate them with water from dams or rivers. The water table rises, as the trees are no longer drawing the massive volumes of water up from the deep soil, at the same time as the amount of water coming into the system is increased as it is constantly applied through irrigation. The soluble salts that exist in the subsoils are brought up with the rising water table. When the water table reaches 2 metres from the surface, the salts are taken up by capillary action, which is wick-like, and deposited in the upper soil, and on top of the soil. Most plants cannot grow in this saline soil, and damage to buildings, roads, pipes also begins. Remaining vegetation dies, and new plants are hard to establish. The cost is vast, ecologically, financially and emotionally, and the repair job is based on experimentation.

With awareness of the movement of materials in the garden environment, the gardener making a decision about how to garden can start to ask, *Where did this come from and where will it go?* This includes the movement of seeds and plant material (that's how weeds spread); of pollen (companies investing in the genetic engineering of plant material find it convenient to forget the pollen flow); of poison (many clever brand names help us ignore the fact that poison travels); of beautiful nectar (through the bodies of birds and the hives of bees); of organic matter (purchased mulch comes in trucks, compost contains manures from farm sheds or racetracks, shredded papers from offices, food scraps from supermarkets); even of flowers and vegetables grown and picked and eaten or given away, over the fence to the neighbour.

Nature is dynamic, it is always on the move. That is as true in the garden environment as in the surging ocean. People, however, often carry an image in their mind of the garden as a fixed thing. They see it as they want it to be, and try to make it stay that way. To these people, the garden can become a battleground. Poisons may bring wings and legs to a stand still *for a while* but wind and water cannot be stilled, and the unseen depths of soil move all the while, imperceptibly and silently. This is part of the nature of the garden as environment, and is important when considering the subtle ways in which our actions and choices affect the environment, the ecology, on both sides of the fence.

I started gardening in the 1970s, a decade when the use of the words 'ecosystem' and 'ecology' entered the mainstream vocabulary. Apparently the word 'ecosystem' was coined in 1935 by A. G. Tansley, first appearing in an article he published in the journal, *Ecology*. So, it is a young word in the scheme of things, although it describes something as old as life itself. In modern Western society, a society which I believe to be nature-impoverished, signs of grave ecological crisis came to light in the 1960s and 1970s, leading to the popularisation of the concept of the web of life, of the interconnectedness of all things. That is, of ecology, of ecosystem. This awareness and understanding has largely been gained through science, although countless experiences of the world ought to tell us that all life is linked. However, very often we do not trust our own perception or intelligence, and prefer to wait on scientific proof. It is this mindset that enables those with a financial or political interest to so often dismiss the warnings of environmentalists as 'emotional'.

It is worth remembering that indigenous people throughout the world have had, and some still have, a deep and thorough knowledge of the natural world around them, as this was a prerequisite for their survival in it. The depth of knowledge held by people who live wholly from the ecosystem they inhabit, without need of outside inputs, is as broad as the knowledge of a scientist specialising in a single species may be narrow. These people may be hunter-gatherers or agrarian. To survive independently in the harshness of Arctic or desert environments depends on intricate knowledge and observation of life's interconnections. To farm sustainably century after century in isolation on the Tibetan plateau, the slopes of the Andes, or anywhere on this Earth, requires close and continuous understanding of the seasons and cycles and flows that govern productivity in a managed ecosystem.

The knowledge that nature works in this interconnected way, and that we are part of the web, was for much of human history simply part of our heritage. David Suzuki's book, *The Wisdom of the Elders*, explores this heritage in detail across the cultures of the world. He writes:

> *At its heart, modern ecology is a continuation of the ancient human quest for a deeper understanding of the often invisible and mysterious web of relationships that connect living things to one another and to their surroundings. Today's infant science of nature's patterns and relations has scarcely begun to unveil the tangles of bonds that exist between the species, forces, and materials of the natural world.* [1]

Perhaps then, in nature-impoverished cultures where understandings that in other times and traditions have been simply part of each generation's heritage, a second chance to understand nature is now available through science. And for those of us who are neither farmers nor hunter-gatherers, but have a patch of land we call a 'garden', there exists the opportunity to use this scientific understanding in a way that is realistic and responsible, by adjusting our approach to gardening based on an awareness of the dynamic ecology that cycles and flows both inside and outside the garden fence. Why it is important for gardeners to make this shift is explored in the next two chapters, by looking firstly at the way we garden and secondly at the key events that have fed into the evolution of the organics movement in the last 35 years. The exploration of the way we garden takes a different angle to the one you might be used to — the angle is nature's point of view.

PART 2

The way

we garden

Thou hast loosed an Act upon the world,
and as a stone thrown into a pool so spread
the consequences thou canst not tell how far.
Words of the Buddhist lama in Rudyard Kipling's *Kim*

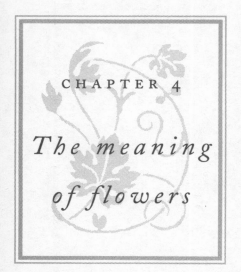

CHAPTER 4

The meaning of flowers

GARDENERS RELATE CHIEFLY TO WHAT GOES ON IN THEIR own gardens. However, as we have seen, gardens are not islands surrounded by a lifeless vacuum. The movement of materials in and out of the garden is not entirely restricted by our fences and walls and boundary lines. Things come and go constantly, without asking permission or knocking or waving farewell. Water, carrying residues of spray or fertiliser, enters and leaves very silently, underground. Air, carrying residues of spray, microscopic spores, grains of pollen, wind-borne seeds, tiny insects, travels ceaselessly across borders; as do ants and birds carrying seeds and aphids carrying disease.

People also come and go, bringing and taking. They bring and take many things, including plants that clever marketing people and garden makeover programs promote like any other consumer good. These media people don't tell you very much. Media time and space are expensive, and information takes time and space. But also, they don't want you to know very much. The media is built around making money, and it is well known that an emotional response is more quickly achieved than the transmission of knowledge. The urge to have something translates easily into product sales.

The things you will read here about the wider implications of the plants you choose are a little complex. It takes time to tell them properly. This chapter is about the effects of your gardening decisions on the world beyond your awareness and beyond your fence. Our vision is very limited. We relate best to what we see and own. The many things we don't see or own, however, are not only important, but often they are fascinating to us, adding a richness and depth to our whole experience of this world, perhaps through indirect perception that is hard to pinpoint. Most people care very much about the consequences of their actions. In order to make an informed choice about decisions in the garden, however, they need to know what those consequences are.

THE PLANTS WE CHOOSE

Ornamental gardening is the dominant form of gardening wherever people have the luxury of not needing to grow their own food. The love of beauty has resulted in plant selection and breeding based on human aesthetics, which as we know are influenced by culture, fashion and personal idiosyncrasies of taste. The Gertrude Jekyll quote in *Chapter 2 — Gardens as we know them* (pp. 23-24) vividly illustrates how an exceptional and incredibly influential garden designer selected and arranged flowerbeds for a painterly effect of colour, texture and composition. The gorgeousness of this art entrances the human mind and emotion, although the perfection of it is out of reach for most gardeners. But I wonder what the insects and birds make of a perfectly contrived Jekyll herbaceous border? I don't really know, but I do know that nature has its own reasons for choosing colours, shapes, sizes and textures in flowers and fruits. These reasons are totally practical. They are to do with sex, reproduction, competition, distribution—in short, survival in an unforgiving world.

The original tones, stripes, spots, colour combinations and shapes of plant parts are adaptations for survival. Adaptations for survival in the impersonal and dynamic process of evolution by natural selection; adaptations for survival in a world of connections and interdependence, of both unconscious competition and the mutually beneficial cooperation of symbiosis. These flowers and fruits that we judge for their visual display, and perhaps for their fragrance, are the food supply, and even the homes, of countless other animal life forms. And the aesthetics that drive our choice of garden plants very often deprive these life forms of their food and homes, making ecological deserts of our charming gardens.

Flowers are the gardener's indulgence and often, their motivation. But for plants, even the most extravagant and bizarre of flowers is an entirely practical invention. Recall for a moment if you can, the voice of David Attenborough, whose gentle tones have described the weirdest and most beautiful of these to us as he gazes enchantingly out of the TV screen. Here is a little of what he writes about in why some plants bother with the gorgeousness of flowers:

> *If a flowering plant is to reproduce sexually, it must ensure that its pollen reaches the style of another individual of the same species ... Those plants that rely on the wind for transport produce small inconspicuous flowers ... Wind is a very effective transporter ... But it is totally haphazard. So the overwhelming proportion of the millions of pollen grains produced by a single plant will fail to reach the stigma of another and therefore be wasted. Since pollen is rich in oils and proteins, and producing it constitutes a significant expense in a plant's economy, this represents a very considerable loss.*

Other plants adopt a different strategy. To reduce the squandering of pollen they invest in devices that recruit animal messengers who collect it and deliver it directly to the female parts of others. A plant will almost certainly be competing with its neighbours of the same species to attract the attention of such messengers. Those that advertise more successfully will leave more offspring, so the competition escalates and over many generations the advertisements become more and more striking ... Among birds this rivalry produces the spectacular plumage of peacocks and birds of paradise. Among plants it has led to the development of glorious flowers.[1]

There are some very careful and strategic arrangements between these 'glorious flowers' and all sorts of animals. These arrangements are part of the food chains and webs in ecosystems, as well as enabling plants to cross-fertilise. Natural flowers are a vital link in the matrix of life that whirls on our planet. Each time a gardener chooses a flowering plant for its appeal to him or herself, the matrix shifts a little further from nature's practical foundation. The original purpose of most flowers is probably irrelevant in most gardens. Gardens have become multicultural. They are congregations of plants from all around the globe that have one thing in common — people like them. Camellias from China, fuchsias from South America, cherry blossoms from Japan, bulbs from Turkey are all commonly found in Australian backyards because we love their glorious flowers. But what role, if any, can they play in the local food chain? Not only are they from far-off lands with different ecologies, by the time they become 'good garden performers' they are most likely the products of artificial selection processes which ignore the needs of the food chains and webs that animate ecosystems. Each and every selected characteristic is there to suit human aesthetics alone. We tend to choose flowers that are showy, colourful, dramatic and long-lasting, aiming for displays that give us pleasure. We know what attracts *us* to flowers, but how aware are we of the colours, shapes and perfumes that attract the myriad other life forms which may have nowhere else to look for their lunch?

THE PALETTE

Colour is the speciality of flowers. You will have noticed that many flowers have a centre of a contrasting colour, such as the black centre of black-eyed Susan and *Rudbeckia* to name only two. The centre may be much darker or much lighter than the outer petals. These contrasting centres are known as the bull's eye, for they appear as a target for insects to home in on. Different insects are attracted to different colour patterns. For example, red and yellow appeal to butterflies, while bees do not see the red end of the spectrum. You will also have noticed that sometimes there are lines radiating out from a flower's centre in a contrasting colour to the main hue of the petals. And there are other lines and patterns that you will *not* have noticed, because the human eye does not see everything.

The human eye sees a limited range of the colour spectrum and some of us don't even see all the colours of the rainbow, due to colour blindness. Ultraviolet light reveals lines and colours invisible to us, but not to the insects that depend on them for the identification of a food source. While bees do not see the red end of the spectrum, their perception at the blue end is much more extensive than ours.

Flowers know and use this knowledge in their eternal quest to attract pollinators. The contrasting centre colours and the radiating lines or spots, whether visible or invisible to us, are guides that attract and lead insects to the nectar and pollen held in the cup of the flower. These lines or spots are known as nectar guides, and they aid insects much as pilots are guided into landing by lines on the tarmac.

The natural colours and patterns of flowers and fruits have a beauty of *purpose* of which we are largely unaware. The evening primrose, for example, appears to us to be a simple pale yellow flower, whose colouring is only slightly stronger towards the centre. Under ultraviolet light, however, strongly coloured pointers radiating from the flower's centre are revealed. They are there to guide pollinators, who have first of all been attracted from a distance by the fragrance carried so sweetly on the night air. As the visitor (in this case a moth) sups nectar, they unwittingly collect pollen grains that hitch a ride to the next flower. In this way, the primrose's genes are spread, and the moth is fed, or paid — for as Attenborough so pithily points out, 'A messenger needs a wage.' The apparently plain blue gentian also shows markings under ultraviolet light, which would be visible to a bee, but are not seen by humans.

And whilst on the subject of blue flowers, why is it that blue is a relatively unusual flower colour in the wild? One theory is that blue is fairly indistinguishable against a green background. And yet the human love of blue means we go to great lengths to breed blue flowers, and covet them in our gardens for their beauty to *our* eye. The quest for a blue rose has, oddly, made it the holy grail of ornamental plant breeders. The achievement of a blue carnation using genetic engineering generated many thousands of advertising dollars for the gardening media. I could tell you stories of unpleasant tussles between advertising people and editors over the ethical dilemma arising from an editorial stance that opposes genetic engineering and the importance of revenue from companies that make these weird plants. But I won't do that here. I'm sure you can imagine it.

Many flowers have important markings that we *do* see. For example, pansies, foxgloves and irises all have stripes or spots that lead to the nectary whose sweet water is only there to give the pollinator a reason to visit. The markings on flowers are part of their beauty to the human eye. The elegance of the iris comes from both its remarkable shape and the loveliness of the colour patterns and contrasts that fan out like splashed paint from the secrecy of the inner tube. The quaintness of foxgloves is likewise a combination of their comfortable shape, soft colours and the carefree look of the spots that seem so absently arranged.

Flower breeding often accentuates one characteristic at the expense of others, based on *human* preferences. For example, my lemon-scented geranium is in the garden because of its fragrant foliage, not its flowers. The flowers are not spectacular to the human eye. They are small, simple, pale pink with thin, dark-hued nectar guides leading to the centre. I have one of these growing beside a sumptuous, large-flowered deep crimson pelargonium. I do not plant pelargoniums but the previous owner of my house had rather a liking for them. Especially pink ones. The lemon-scented and the velvety-crimson stunner were the only two that I kept, one because of my weakness for lemon-scented foliage, the other because of its drama when in flower. I have stood and watched as bees home in again and again on the simple but practical flowers of the lemon-scented, while not one bee takes a jot of notice of *my* floral preference, the royal-rich crimson. If not for the lemon-scented, the bees and hoverflies would be elsewhere, or hungry. When plant breeders select for new 'improved' colours, they affect these subtle, time-tested arrangements between plant and pollinator, depriving fauna of food, and rendering the plant sterile or dependent on self-fertilisation, which inhibits genetic diversity, a major disadvantage in the evolution stakes.

While horticulturalists and marketing companies gloat over peculiar contrivances such as genetically engineered blue carnations, enormous pansies and striped roses, they give no thought to the meaning of these colours and shapes to birds and insects. I used to work in the gardening media. I remember much excitement about striped roses (at least in gardening magazines dependent on dramatic floral fashions and photography for achieving sales figures attractive to advertisers). I have wondered if these theatrical circus-tent stripes waste the often finely balanced energy of insects that are attracted by them and in search of a feed, only to find that the flower is all talk and no substance. For all too often these highly bred flowers are sterile, lacking the pollen and nectar which birds and insects feed on. Or if it *is* there, it may be quite inaccessible, buried in a maze of petals that are layered like the flounces on a ball gown such as in glamorously advertised double- and triple-petalled flowers like roses and camellias.

MATTERS OF SIZE

I have already mentioned pansies in relation to their colour and the guidelines that lead insects to their centre. Pansies are the most popular autumn bedding annual in Australia. Each season there are new varieties to tempt us with their colour schemes and upturned faces. As well as colour, another preoccupation ornamental plant breeders have is with size.

I recall a few years ago the showy marketing campaign that went with the 'world's largest pansy'. This enormous flop-eared flower with its great rounded petals was a novelty to titillate consumers. However, the oversized petals would have had no strength as a landing platform for a hungry insect. One function of petals is to provide a stable resting place for feeding insects who must cope with al fresco dining conditions. It would take only a light breeze to lift the sail-like petals of the world's largest pansy, destabilising all six legs of any insect that had managed to gain a foothold in the first place. Without the correct colours, the guidelines and the perfume, the insects probably wouldn't have found the flower anyway, and even if they had stumbled and bumbled into what nature would regard as a uselessly deformed bloom, the cupboard may well have been bare, as the need for nectar and pollen is a sexual one, and these flowers are all show and no action — sterile hybrids which exist only because of human cleverness and the economy of the ornamental horticulture industry. They have been manufactured, and when the factory stops making them, they will no longer exist. From the point of view of nature, which is eternally opportunistic, they are a waste of space. They are barren to themselves and to other life.

Perfectly perfumed

Perfume is another thing. Insects have an excellent sense of smell, though birds do not.

The loss of fragrance in breeding flowers such as sweet pea, *Lathyrus odoratus*, is another example of carelessness when it comes to appreciating and respecting the role played by the natural qualities of flowers.

The bee is the main pollinator of sweet pea. Bees are attracted by particular colour patterns and also by scent. The sweet pea originated in Sicily and southern Italy where the straggly vines supported two small flowers per stem as they sprawled under the Sicilian sun. The little blooms were coloured a dark, brooding blue-purple and a dense, deep claret. From these unremarkable-looking flowers drifted a remarkably strong, sweet scent. Seeds were first sent to England in 1699 where they were grown primarily for their fragrance until the plant breeders of the late 19th and early 20th centuries used artificial cross-pollination to develop larger flowers, new colours and most famously, frilled petals. In this quest for size, colour and frilliness, they lost the original, enigmatic feature of the flower — its fragrance.

They also paid no regard to the importance of the original shape to visiting insects, let alone colour. Pea flowers are a complex shape, looking something like a butterfly. There is a sort of keel or shelf where a pollinating insect can land. From there it must reach into the flower's centre for a sip of nectar. As it does so, its weight presses down in such a way that the pollen-covered stigma darts out, rubbing pollen along the body of the visitor. The insect takes its sup of nectar and leaves, carrying a dusting of pollen grains like lipstick on the cheek of a man who does not know he is marked. At the next flower visited there is a pollen *exchange*, as the sticky stigma both collects and deposits the yellow grains.

Sadly, the large, frilly, variously coloured garden flowers may have little or nothing to offer a hungry insect for several reasons, as has been seen in both the pansy and the sweet pea. Both the visual and olfactory cues for finding them in the first place have been compromised. The size and shape of petals and sexual parts may no longer facilitate feeding — the specifically developed proportions of the original flower for insect feeding and pollen distribution no longer exist. The quantity of nectar and pollen in hybrid blooms may be very low, so even if they are visited, there is little reward. The flower has lost its sexuality, and with it a food source for those insects it depended on for pollen transport.

In breeding flowers to please the human aesthetic in this way, they become little more than garden ornaments for the gratification of the 'owner'. It should be acknowledged that efforts have been made to bring back the sweetness to the sweet pea, but it is still the old-fashioned, less showy varieties that have the strongest scent. They are the ones for the ecologically minded gardener to choose.

As with colour, the range of scents detectable by humans and insects varies. Many odours that attract insects simply cannot be smelled by people. So even though we may choose to plant perfumed flowers, and breeders may try to bring back the scent of flowers such as sweet pea and roses, there will be many subtle plant—animal interactions based on odour that we are completely unaware of.

Of the odours that we do notice, some are sweet, while others may be repulsive to us. If a flower smells of urine or rotting flesh, we are unlikely to want it in our gardens. However, if your pollinator is a fly or ant, these smells are there for a reason. I am not suggesting that to be a responsible eco-gardener you must plant putrid-smelling flowers, I'm simply making the point that everything in nature has a good reason for being the way it is, and each time we humans make choices based on our own aesthetic tastes, we disadvantage one or more other species. As human dominance of the planet increases, the impact of these choices also increases.

Of all the specific plant and animal interactions, perhaps the most graphic illustrations of finely tuned adaptations are found amongst the weird things that happen between orchids and their chosen insects. These are without doubt the most intriguing, bizarre and efficient pollination strategies anywhere in the vastness of the plant kingdom.

The *Orchidaceae* is the most diverse and highly evolved of any plant family. Its approximately 30 000 species make up 10 percent of all flowering plants. Orchids grow the world over, in habitats that range from totally underground (Western Australia) to high in the canopy of jungle trees, and almost everywhere hot, cold, dry, moist, light, dark or in-between. They are a recently evolved plant group which are highly complex, and you could say, devious. Many orchids, rather than developing mutually beneficial relationships with the insect world, have found ways of using the insects for their own means and basically making fools of them. In *The Secret Life of Plants*, David Attenborough writes:

> *Plants reward all kinds of animals — bats and birds and overwhelmingly, insects — for carrying their pollen. The arrangement seems fair. But there is no morality in the natural world and there are plants that achieve the same result without rewarding their couriers in any way. Indeed, some trap and seemingly punish them. Orchids, in particular, have developed a range of enticements that in the event provide no reward whatsoever for those that succumb.* [2]

These clever flowers, often highly feminine in appearance, tend to use the desires of male insects to achieve their own reproductive ends. One South American group, known as dancing lady orchids *Oncidium*, send out a spray of tiny flowers on little stalks. They dance and shiver in the breeze, looking like a swarm of fine insects. A stroppy little bee shares the same forest neighbourhood. The males are extremely territorial. When they come across these delicate orchids, they attack, intending to send the intruders packing. As they do so, they gather a load of pollen which they unwittingly distribute each time they do useless battle in this way.

More kinky than these dancing girls are the orchids that tempt male insects to copulate with their flower. This is done by both visual mimicry of the female and the production of a scent resembling pheromones secreted by female insects to attract mates. The males come along believing they've found the girl they are after, as the orchid looks and smells like the mate he seeks. In their eagerness, they land on the flower and attempt to copulate. They fail, of course, but in the process the orchid loads them up with pollen that they carry on to another impostor, fulfilling the sexual need of the plant rather than that of themselves. Each species of orchid that uses this cunning ploy has one specific bee or wasp that it has worked out how to trick, without whom, the orchid cannot mate.

In the darkness of night

The garden at night supports another dimension of nature of which we have little awareness. Producing a fragrance takes energy, so flowers are only fragrant when it is useful to them to be so. Plants pollinated by birds and butterflies don't bother with scent, as these pollinators have a poor sense of smell. So too, flowers pollinated by bees will not be highly fragrant in the afternoon or night, as morning is the time of greatest bee activity. Many insects, however, do come out at night.

Pale colours and a strong fragrance are typical of flowers that wish to attract night flyers. The pathway through the dark is lit by large, pale flowers whose perfume is part of the living map that guides night-feeders to seemingly dull shrubs which awaken at night. The timing of fragrance is controlled by the plant's sensitivity to light. If moths or bats are the preferred agent, night is the time to advertise one's existence.

Some plant species have taken their nocturnal habits to extremes. During the day the flowers of the night-scented jasmine *Cestrum nocturnum* look half dead. As the light fades, they come to life, filling the darkness with a fragrance, much like a neon light advertising that this night-spot is now open for drinks. It is not a great looking shrub, however, and with the human preference for visual gratification, the attractions of plants like this to nightlife are commonly overlooked by design-conscious gardeners. With these self-centred humans in control, where are the night fliers to get a good feed?

The liaison between a night-scented orchid and a particularly long-snouted moth in Madagascar is unlikely to be affected by the plant selection of most gardeners. But as an illustration of the many singular and mostly unseen dances of the night, the 'monogamy' of this moth and this orchid is a supreme example.

The flower is a large, creamy white star with a nectar-holding spur that trails an unlikely 20–35 cm. Its name, almost as long as the spur, is descriptive—*Angraecum sesquipedale*. The species name, *sesquipedale*, means 'a foot-and-a-half'. Its pollinator is a hawkmoth with an even longer title—*Xanthopan morgani forma praedicta*, and a proboscis to match the orchid's spur. This remarkable proboscis, which is kept coiled beneath the moth's head, is able to dip down deep into the nectary as the moth hovers alongside in the warm night air. The flower has no scent during the day, but with darkness comes a powerful perfume that lasts until morning. This moth is its only pollinator. Madagascar must be a wonder-ful place for a naturalist. I am continually coming across odd and extreme examples of plant–animal relationships that happen there, and you will read more of these later.

Under cover of darkness, insects are not the only night-fliers looking for food. Not all bats are blind, and the larger species, the flower and fruit feeders, are important pollinators in both rainforests and deserts. Pale, perfumed flowers that glow in the moonlight offer both nectar and pollen to these large-eyed bats. As both their habitat and their food supplies shrink, fruit bats are sometimes regarded as pests. They fly out at night, 'raiding' orchards. They live in dense populations in forest remnants or botanical gardens where the stench of their guano, their restless noises and the damage they do to trees and understorey make them unpopular with nearby residents.

I spent seven years living in the subtropics. Two kilometres down the road was a flying fox colony. I loved to watch them at dusk as they flew out of town in their thousands, it seemed, to search for food, animating the evening sky. When my guavas and native figs were in fruit, the sound of their flapping and chatter in the trees was like a layer of the night. There was also a night-scented jasmine by the door, and in the warm, still darkness the air lived, vivid with perfume, dense with the presence of the bats. The porch light was thick with insects, a green tree frog stuck to the wall to feast on them.

I used to take people on night walks in a nearby rainforest national park. The flying foxes were there too, in the treetops amongst the lush, out-of-reach flowers of giants that bloom only occasionally and extravagantly and need the bats to pollinate them. I planted native trees that would provide food for these bats, and it saddens me to think of that fecund valley without the fruit bats, should their habitat fail. Their base was confined to one small island of weed-infested rainforest in a rural river valley that was once all jungle. This island, known simply as Bat Island, was visited weekly (and probably still is) by a small dedicated group of bush regenerators, whose patient weeding and planting kept the native ecosystem viable. Without the flying foxes, the giant rainforest trees that depend on their services as pollinators will not set seed and over time, they also will die out. To see these flying mammals feasting noisily in the lush rainforest canopy of nearby Dorrigo National Park is to observe the dynamism, interdependence, and *independence* of nature simply getting on with life. How can we be so one-eyed as to call them pests? Who is the pest? Have the bats destroyed our homes? Are we not clever enough, in all our cleverness, to keep them off our orchards?

Instead of calling them 'pests', we can plant food for them; the food they have evolved to live on which we have cleared and replaced with orchards and exotic gardens. When they come to feed on your 'bat' plantings, I have no doubt that you will appreciate their mysterious beauty and purpose as they party the night away in your friendly garden. Their guano will nourish the soil and they will trade in pollen, taking the genes from your plantings to other gardens and parks and forests. Fruit will then set, and in its turn feed an array of birds, insects, bats, fungi, marsupials, all of whom are linked to other life forms in other ways, and who may help spread the seeds so that forests continue to be renewed, cleaning and manufacturing the very air we breathe.

There is no isolation, there is no separation. Each organism is a piece in the jigsaw puzzle, and with each extinction, the picture diminishes and makes less sense.

There is much more to see on that night walk. In the blackness of the night garden is the lushness of jungle and the partying of bats, again highlighting the garden as a place that travellers pass through for refreshment and sustenance, heedless of boundary lines and fences. So many creatures and plants have not been mentioned. Night-weaving spiders who eat their webs at dawn; small and giant moths brilliantly camouflaged and invisible by day; singing crickets calling for lovers; deeply-fragrant pittosporums and the other heady perfumes that pervade all in the cool and damp and secret-feeling night.

It is all too easy for gardeners to be unaware of the ecological importance of what happens in their garden at night. Gardens are generally planted for enjoyment under the sun. The only area that might rate some attention for its night-time appeal is the outdoor entertainment area. In this zone, we are more likely to be thinking about how to repel insects than attract them. The fashion for using spotlights to highlight visual features of the garden is likewise based around a human aesthetic with little consideration given to the sensitivity of nocturnal plants and animals to artificial lighting. Our understanding seldom goes further than realising that light attracts insects. What are the repercussions of this? And what of the creatures who may be repelled by light, or the plants whose highly tuned sensors respond to varying levels of light intensity, be they of the moon, the sun or a floodlight? The life cycles of many plants and animals are affected by the cycles of the moon, and by day length. These are indicators that tell when conditions are favourable for certain activities. There is already so much light pollution in towns and cities that night has developed a permanent glow. Garden lighting compounds this loss of darkness.

Every choice made by the gardener has a consequence. Whilst making that choice, consider the life forms that were there before you, but may not be there as a result of your choices.

Flamboyance is for the birds

Birds are another story altogether. What do they care for sexy perfumes and slinky lines that need strange eyes or UV contrivances just to be seen? This is all too subtle for their tastes. Give them big red flowers dripping nectar and a strong stalk to grip onto, and they will take pollen to your neighbour, no questions asked. Think of the Australian grevilleas, kangaroo paw, bottle brush and most magnificent, the NSW waratah — radiant, sturdy, nectar-rich and with pollen strategically placed for brushing onto the bird's head or neck. Very often, these flowers hold their nectar in a deep tube, with the pollen-carrying stamens held out on long stalks so that they are in the way, ensuring contact is made with the bird as it dives in for a drink. The white waratah is coveted as a rarity, and considerable effort has gone into breeding white cultivars for sale. Now you know why it is rare — in nature, its whiteness is a disadvantage. It is bird-pollinated and birds love red, not white. So if you love the sight of honeyeaters dunking their fine beaks hungrily into the incredible inflorescence of the waratah, plant red ones, not white.

As with the moth and orchid in Madagascar, some birds and flowers are totally interdependent, with only one species of bird capable of pollinating a certain species of plant. Perhaps the most delightful, hard-working and specialised of the nectar-feeding birds are the South

American hummingbirds. These tiny birds do not need a stalk to grip or a landing platform at all. Their wings can beat so fast, and their skill at positioning is so accurate, that they can hang below a flower and feed from mid-air, their beaks inserted up into the bell-like blossom. Pollen-bearing stamens hang down from the petals, brushing against the bird's chin as it feeds. Once again, I will let David Attenborough elaborate on the precision of the relationship:

> *South American plants ... attract them with delicate flowers, suspended from the end of long thin stems and facing outwards so that they can only be entered from the air. The rate at which such a flower supplies its nectar has to be carefully controlled. If the plant is miserly and produces very little, a bird will not find it worthwhile calling. If it is too generous, then the bird might be so satisfied after its visit that it will not hurry to seek more nectar elsewhere and so fail to deliver the pollen swiftly. Many plants have arrived at such a perfect compromise between these two extremes that the hummingbirds pollinating them are compelled to keep continuously active, rushing from one flower to another, getting just enough each time to fuel their high-energy flying equipment with just sufficient calories left over to make the trip profitable. At night, when they cannot see to fly and the flowers have closed, the birds have no alternative but to shut down all their systems, lower their body temperature and, in effect, hibernate until dawn.*[3]

Aquilegia are one such flower visited by hummingbirds. I have some hybrids growing in my Hobart garden. We also call them columbine, and granny's bonnet. The stalks of my hybrids are strong and upright. The flowers do not droop delicately. There are no hummingbirds here looking for a meal, it is true. I speak hypothetically, imagining I am a gardener in South America, where I have never been. I have planted hybrid aquilegia, whose flowers are arranged for human needs, such as garden display, colour preference or cut-flower arrangement. If a hummingbird came, with its high demands for constant food, my pretty hybrids may not meet its needs. I suspect it would not come again and my garden would be the duller, and the hummingbird population possibly smaller, as a result.

Australia has a predominance of nectar-feeding birds. Globally, most nectar-feeders live in the tropics, as they need a year-round supply of flowers. Of the 151 species of honeyeaters known on Earth, 73 are found in Australia, where they dwell in all manner of habitats, from arid areas to tropical rainforest. Eighty percent of these birds are nomadic, following the flowering of native plants. In Australia, where climates range from the temperate to the tropical, they make their way gradually from north to south and south to north, as the seasons change and the flowering moves location. As natural areas dwindle, the importance of environmentally sensitive gardening increases. If you plant with these birds in mind, their journey will be easier, and your garden will be animated by their bright presence.

As we already know, many of the highly bred flowers lack both the nectaries and the floral structure needed for bird and insect feeding. The importance of planting simple and 'old-fashioned' species, both native and exotic, cannot be over emphasised. The honeyeaters need long-blooming plants that flower in succession for as many months as possible.

In Australia, the grevilleas, banksias, callistemons, melaleucas and gums are just a few indigenous genera that produce an abundance of nectar across the seasons. Plant the species that belong to your area, with some attention to spreading the flowering times, and the birds will home in. These birds also help maintain the ecological balance of your garden. Although they are nectar feeders, many of them depend largely on a diet of insects which are essential to their young, whose rapid development requires a high-protein, low-fat diet.

OTHER CREATURES WHO VISIT FLOWERS

Reptiles may also have close relationships with flowers. In New Zealand there is a wide-eyed gecko with a contented smile. It feeds at night on the nectar of native flax flowers. It is a messy feeder and comes away with its throat covered in yellow pollen grains. These, of course, brush off on other flax flowers, and in this way the genetic diversity of the flax plants is maintained.

Some small mammals also feed on nectar. In Australia, pygmy and honey possums sup the nectar of gum blossom and other nectar-rich flowers, transferring pollen via their fur as they go between plants. In southern Africa, some species of protea provide a night feast of nectar for small rock mice and shrews. Again, pollen, the world's most adept hitchhiker, catches a ride.

The traveller's palm *Ravenala madagascariensis*, with its huge, vertical, fan-shaped leaves, is a popular ornamental in warm-climate gardens. It comes from Madagascar, also home to the ruffed lemur. The clusters of flowers have large nectar chambers which provide the main food of the lemur during flowering season. The lemur has hands that can pull apart the protective bracts that surround the flowers and teeth which are needed to open the flower itself. It also has an extra long snout and tongue, enabling it to reach and drink the nectar. It is thought that palm and lemur have evolved together, as no other creature seems to have the wherewithal to access this nectar.

These examples of interdependence between plants and animals show how finely balanced many ecological relationships are, and indicate the problems that can arise from people tinkering with flowers. Some of these are certainly extreme examples, which are not available to gardeners. Nevertheless, I hope that this information, though bits of it are rather exotic, highlights the need for gardeners to respect plant—animal relationships if they wish for their gardening to contribute to the health of local biodiversity and ecology.

Of course there are going to be many such relationships that gardeners will not know about specifically, and there is no need to. If the principles of gardening for biodiversity are used, then most of the interactions between the plant and animal kingdoms will happen without the gardener's knowledge or involvement, simply because we have provided the opportunity for them to happen. But if the garden is based purely on the owner's aesthetics or gardening fashions, then the chance for a diverse ecology to exist there will be a hit-and-miss business. The need for fauna to feed is constant. If food is not available, they move out or die out. They cannot wait for fashion to favour their feeding habits. No, they need an ongoing and reliable food source, as well as somewhere suitable to live and breed, just as we do. Australia's nectar-feeding birds, traversing this wide brown land in their dependence on the nectar flow of flowers, are a good example.

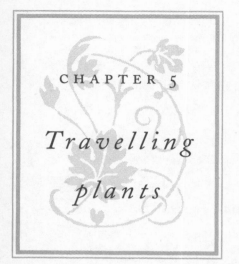

CHAPTER 5

Travelling plants

THE TERM *GARDEN ESCAPES* SAYS A LOT MORE THAN THE word *weed*, for it implies that a garden is a confined area of land. It implies that the boundaries set by humans should be recognised and respected by other life forms. If a plant 'escapes', has the plant misbehaved, like a person or animal who *escapes* (presumably from captivity)? Are fences expected to be cage walls that keep all within them from 'escaping'? With this fortress mentality, expressed by our very language, have we forgotten that the wind blows free over and through fences, and that light-as-air seeds fly with the wandering wind? Have we forgotten that insects, birds, bats, even mammals, who are not captive, eat and collect seeds and fruit in our gardens, then defecate elsewhere, their droppings containing fertiliser-encapsulated seeds whose dormancy has been broken by digestion? Or that pollinators trade in pollen, thus carrying genes selected for garden performance into the wild populations of native plants, leading to so-called 'genetic pollution'?

The potential repercussions of genetic pollution are multiplying with the introduction of genetic engineering. Pollinators carry the modified pollen, which may include the 'terminator' gene or genes with insecticidal properties, from crops to closely related non-crop populations. The terminator gene makes the plant's seed unviable. It is designed for purely commercial reasons. By stopping growers from collecting their own seed they are forced into dependence on seed merchants, with all the sinister repercussions of monopoly. That is not our direct concern here. The issue here is genetic pollution. The scenario is one in which the terminator gene is transferred by pollination to wild populations of related plants. The seeds of these wild plants will become useless. The plants will be unable to reproduce. Plant families such as the Brassicaceae have many members that are grown commercially, plus many close relatives used in ornamental horticulture, and yet others which grow wild. The potential for 'designer' genes to spread through this clan is obvious.

WHEN THE GARDEN ESCAPES

Within Australian gardens, farms and bushland there are many weeds that were introduced into this country as garden ornamentals and shelter plants for farms. And it is not all in the past. New plants continue to be introduced, and others that may have behaved well for many years can suddenly go stir-crazy and want out — this personality change may be caused by the arrival of a pollinator or seed vector that makes them fertile, the loss of an agent that kept them under control, or simply by a weather event that favours their reproduction and spread. These potential pests (not only plants) are known as 'sleepers', and may take more than 100 years to wake from their deceptively peaceful slumber. Given Australia's relatively short gardening history, this is very bad news.

An irritatingly avoidable example of this is the way pampas grass *Cortaderia selloana* became weedy in mainland Australia, and latterly in Tasmania after almost 100 years. The pampas has two types of plants — female and hermaphrodite. On the hermaphrodite plants, however, the female parts are sterile. The females have larger, more attractive plumes, so they are preferred as a garden ornamental. Initially only female clones with white plumes were planted, both on mainland Australia and in Tasmania, thus ensuring high quality, non-invasive plantings. Without her mate, the pampas did not stray. As well as being a dramatic and beautiful garden plant, she was useful on farms as shelter for lambs and as a soil stabiliser, especially on light, sandy soils. All was well until seeds of a softly coloured form were imported for ornamental variety. These hermaphrodite seedlings spread their pollen, and in the 1970s, pampas suddenly became a major problem on the mainland.

Meanwhile, Tasmania's isolation protected it—for the time being. However, someone wanting to raise cheap plants for mass-use brought in seeds, thus introducing males onto the island. Wind pollinated, and with seeds spread by wind and water, pampas quickly became a serious environmental weed on this windy island of water courses. It should be noted that there is another species of *Cortaderia* which is asexually self-fertile. That is, its female flowers are able to set seed without pollination. Not as attractive as *C. selloana*, *C. jubata* is often mistakenly referred to (and sold by nurseries) as pampas grass. It is more correctly called jubata grass, and if anything, is a more serious weed than pampas in many parts of the world.

Gloriosa superba is a beautiful and inspiring name for a plant. It belongs to the glory lily, whose bright orange blooms and vigorous habit make it attractive to gardeners. 'Bullet-proof' plants is a theme that gardening writers and television presenters constantly return to in their quest to engage the interest of non-gardeners and gardeners in search of 'low-maintenance' plants. The glory lily has no doubt been on their list. It is a spectacular vine that grows from bulbs, thriving in sun or shade. Every part of the plant is toxic, including the seeds, protecting it from pest attack. It grows as happily in the salty, low-nutrient 'soil' of sand dunes as it does in the rich humus of littoral (coastal) rainforest. It propagates by seed, multiplication of bulbs, layering and stem cuttings, sending out adventitious roots from any leaf node that contacts a moist medium. A NSW National Parks and Wildlife Service media release from 2004 reports that the glory lily 'has now become one of the most serious environmental weeds on the north coast of NSW'.[1] Dense infestations of up to 100 stems per square metre grow from the mass of tubers spreading in the loose, warm soil, while the vines climb for up to 4 metres, smothering the natural vegetation. So-called bullet proof plants have the potential to become highly invasive environmental weeds, threatening the biodiversity of ecosystems and placing further demand on human resources of time, energy and money.

Gardeners should be wary of exotic plants that are promoted as 'bullet-proof', or 'thrive on neglect'. The key question to ask is, what are *their reproductive strategies*? If they reproduce easily and quickly, it is only a matter of time before they escape. Such plants have no place in an environmentally responsible garden. Ironically, botanical gardens are prime suspects when it comes to harbouring sleepers. They are collections of plants from all over the world. In his startling book, *Feral Future*, Tim Low writes:

> *Botanic gardens are, in effect, zoos for plants, but with no cages to confine the exhibits … Vast assortments of weird and wonderful species are kept under minimal security. The number of plants grown can be enormous. Adelaide Botanic Gardens was growing more than 8,000 species back in 1878.*

Many of these plants are so obscure we know nothing about their prospects as weeds.[2]

Mimosa bush *Mimosa pigra*, a weed whose massive invasion of Australia's Top End threatens Kakadu National Park, was originally imported by the Darwin Botanic Gardens in the late 1800s. This weed was a sleeper until several extreme wet seasons in the 1970s carried its floating seedpods to the Adelaide River flood plain. The ability of each plant to produce around 200 000 seeds per year meant that within just three decades, dense thickets of mimosa were strangling 800 square km of wetland, displacing important and complex native ecologies. With the capacity to double its territory each year, this so-called sensitive plant (its ferny leaves recoil remarkably from touch) sleeps no more. It is now very wide awake, and playing hide-and-seek with full-time teams whose mission is to find and destroy mimosa's advance on Kakadu in particular.

There are plenty of other examples of botanic garden escapes and of single plants held in botanic gardens' collections which are regarded suspiciously by those with an eye for plants with weed potential.

Gardeners have a responsibility to educate themselves about what not to plant. In Australia, this is not hard to do. Most local councils have pamphlets listing known garden escapes. Many councils have Bushcare coordinators on staff, with bushland management plans in place. These people work hard to reduce the impact of environmental weeds on bushland remnants. They have researched control strategies and generally adopt a long-term approach that gives the bush a chance to heal itself. Much has been learned in the last 30–40 years about bush regeneration in Australia.

Sadly, commercial nurseries cannot be relied upon to give accurate or honest advice about plants with weed potential. I learned this from personal experience in the early 1980s when I was employed on a research-oriented bush regeneration project on the Queens Domain in Hobart. The Domain is a precious remnant of native grassland adjacent to central Hobart. One weed I became all too familiar with was *Acacia pycnantha*, the golden wattle—Australia's floral emblem. Understandably, I was disturbed to see this plant being sold by a native plant nursery at Hobart's popular Salamanca Market. I was even more disturbed, however, by the stall holder's defensive, almost aggressive response when I explained that I was paid by Hobart City Council to remove these plants from an endangered plant community only a couple of kilometres from where we stood.

Since those days the nursery industry as a whole has certainly taken this issue on board, and there are many environmentally aware and responsible nurserymen and women out there. But you cannot rely on it. Even Australia's most prestigious gardening event, the Melbourne International Flower and Garden Show, has been under the microscope following reports from weed experts about the number of exhibits utilising weed species. By contrast, in Sydney the ABC's *Gardening Australia Live* has attempted to raise the bar by obtaining weed-free certification from the relevant authorities before opening its doors each year.

WEEDS IN THEIR OWN LAND

The example of the weediness of Australia's floral emblem is an important one which raises the issue of the responsible use of 'native plants'. During the 1970s Australians embraced the use of native plants in gardens on a greater scale than ever before. The planting of naturalistic 'bush gardens' became popular as a nation still emerging from its colonial past and from post-war conservatism searched for ways to express an independent and unique identity. The native plants and the bush garden design were said to be 'low maintenance', a direct contrast with the demands of English-style gardens in the harsh climates and low-fertility soils of much of Australia. A native plant was simply thought to be one that grew somewhere in Australia before European arrival. Little or no selection had been done for garden performance, so nursery plants were mainly seedlings of species with all the variety and fertility that produces. Virtually no thought was given to the potential of these plants to become weeds. How could they be a weed in their own land?

Quite easily, as it turned out. For while Australia is one land in terms of its national government and as a continental landmass (although there are also many islands, Tasmania being the largest), it is vast and varied in its ecologies. The east and west and the north and south are separated by arid lands and desert which may as well be sea in terms of their role as geographic boundaries inhibiting the movement of plant and animal species. Ecologically, it therefore makes more sense to distinguish between bioregions rather than using the artificial concept of one-nation or even state boundaries to identify plant groupings. There are all too many examples of 'native' plants going feral within Australia, and becoming invasive environmental weeds.

Wattles are prime candidates. As pioneer plants, their role in nature is to establish quickly after disturbance such as fire or landslip. They stabilise the soil and create nursery conditions in which slower-growing, longer-lived plants can germinate. However, this ability to colonise can become a negative when they are introduced to new areas. The spectacular, and hence popular *Acacia baileyana* (Cootamundra wattle), is one of Australia's most widespread native environmental weeds, displacing local, less competitive species in all Australian states. Ironically, it is now rare at its original address in north-western NSW. Wattles have also proved highly invasive in many other parts of the world. Some species of the genera *Grevillea*, *Eucalyptus*, *Hakea*, *Leptospermum*, *Pittosporum* and *Melaleuca* are other well-known Australians that have become troublesome as environmental weeds in their own country, and in some cases, internationally.

PLANT MINING

As yin has yang, the problem of garden escapes has its opposite. While garden plantings can lead to the invasion of wild ecologies by plants that do not respect fence lines, the desires of gardeners can also *endanger* the wild populations of plants — I am talking about the problem of plants being collected from their wild habitats for sale to the gardening public. Most gardeners don't think about it, because they don't even know that it happens. However, from the time of the Victorian plant collectors to the present day, there are several startling examples of wild places being ruthlessly stripped of plant species that can be dug up, transported and sold to gardeners in far-off lands.

Usually the gardener is an innocent accessory, unwittingly supporting an opportunistic money-making venture of which he or she has no knowledge. There are two players at the buying end of this game — the ordinary gardener who buys plant material with no inkling of its origins, and the obsessive collector who doesn't care where a rare specimen comes from, as long as he can own it. At the selling end of this game, there are also generally two players, each with their own agenda—the opportunistic entrepreneur for whom quick dollars are the obsession, rather than plants, and the gatherers of the plants from the wild, who are often poor village people in remote parts of the world.

Gardeners are curious people. The gardens of gardeners—as opposed to the gardens of non-gardeners (for there are many of these)—are likely to hold within their boundaries at least a few curiosities from the vast and diverse plant kingdom of this planet. To love plants is to want them, and there are so many possibilities. Gardeners are often proudest of the most unusual or rarest or hard-to-grow of the plants in their care. The gardens of plant enthusiasts become collections, with some people falling so much in love with a single plant type that they become a *collector*, striving to own as many different species, cultivars and/or hybrids as possible. This is particularly so with the strange and exotic, such as orchids, carnivorous plants, cacti, succulents and bulbs.

The plant hunters of the age of exploration, and particularly the Victorian era, were hardy adventurers, some of whom have become legends, remembered both for the plants of horticultural and botanical significance that they introduced to the West, and for their endurance in isolated and extreme parts of the globe. There were the botanists on voyages of exploration, such as Joseph Banks, whose interests were scientific and to a lesser extent commercial, and there were horti-culturalists working for nurserymen. The botanists collected herbarium samples and some living plant material. The nurserymen are the ones that concern us here. Their brief was to scour new lands for plants that either had good garden potential or would fetch a high price from wealthy collectors. Coming across a desirable plant in flower, these sharp-witted, intrepid individuals would take careful note and return months later to collect seeds. The world was their oyster, brimful of continents whose mantle of green was rich with vegetation unknown in the gardens and conservatories of England and Europe. The wealthy owners of these gardens and conservatories were hungry for novelty and exotica. Floral treasures from China, India, South Africa, the Americas and Oceania were prizes that fortunes could be made from. Sometimes, however, seeds were not available, so whole plants were taken. Occasionally, entire plant populations were taken, leaving none for competitors and thereby achieving a monopoly.

Orchids seem always to be found at the extreme end of botanical and horticultural lore, their surreal beauty and endless variety ensuring they hold a special place in the human psyche, resulting in some very odd behaviour. The mania for orchids that took hold of Victorian England gives the most graphic and destructive examples of human greed I have come across in the subculture of gardening. The incredibly high prices being paid for rare orchids led to a botanical version of gold-fever. Forests were felled in the gathering of epiphytic orchids that grew on the branches of the upper canopy. In her book, *A History of the Orchid*, Merle A. Reinikka describes the madness as leaving whole areas devastated 'as if by forest fires'. She writes, 'on one particular search for *Odontoglossum crispum* in Colombia, 10 000 plants were collected with the result that 4,000 trees were felled … As one area was stripped and the native vegetation ruined, the collector moved forward week by week, hacking down trees and depleting the natural wealth of orchids.'[3]

A letter from one such collector has become infamous for its honest account of this vandalism. In 1895, Carl Johannsen wrote from Columbia to his English employer:

> *I shall despatch tomorrow 30 boxes, 12 of which contain the finest of all the* Aureas, *the* Monte coromes *form, and 18 cases containing the great* Sanderiana *type all collected from the spot where they grow mixed, and I shall clear them out. They are now extinguished in this spot and this will surely be the last season. I have finished all along the Rio Dagua where there are no plants left; the last days I remained in that spot the people brought in two or three plants at a time and some came back without a single plant.*[4]

Many of the plants perished on their journey across the Atlantic, pushing up the value of those that survived even more. Back in England, at auction, tiny plants of new varieties fetched more than 1000 guineas. Not since 'tulip-mania' gripped 17th-century Europe, with investors spending the equivalent of US$50 000 on a single rare bulb, had plants excited such hip-pocket passion.

Orchid poaching continues to be a problem, although these days it is a black-market operation. Those without conscience will always exploit, but of more relevance to us are the deceptions that honest, well-intentioned gardeners are susceptible to. The most disturbing example of this belongs not to the bric-a-brac world of Victorian England, but to the late 20th century.

EXTINCT FLOWERS FOR SALE

Alarm bells rang in 1985 when a plant expert noticed that a supposedly extinct flower was available for sale in large quantities in the UK. It was *Cyclamen mirabile*, and it had last been recorded in south-eastern Turkey in the 1960s, when over-cultivation was thought to have since wiped it out. Where were all these rare bulbs coming from? Their appearance on the open market prompted conservationists to investigate the wild-bulb trade, whose epicentre is in Holland. An exposé revealed that hundreds of millions of wild-harvested bulbs from Turkey, Greece, Georgia, Hungary and other parts of the Middle East and Central Asia were being sold to gardeners in Europe, the UK and the USA, many of them labelled 'nursery grown from the Netherlands'. As well as several species of cyclamen, there were all sorts of other bulbs such as *Galanthus* (snowdrop), *Anemone*, *Eranthis* (winter aconite) and *Sternbergia* (autumn crocus). Collection of vast numbers of the giant snowdrop *Galanthus elwesii*, have put this species at risk in the wild.

Wild bulbs, including tulips, have been harvested in large quantities from the hills of Turkey for hundreds of years. Turkey's harsh, dry environment has fostered the evolution of an abundance of unique and beautiful flowers, with bulbs that enable them to survive in a dormant state during the most inhospitable time of year. During the 1970s and 1980s many flowers that were previously unknown in the West were 'discovered'. Gardeners love novelty as well as beauty, and the demand for these plants proved a bonanza for the middle-men who organised their collection.

From 1979 to 1989, 564 million bulbs were collected and exported from Turkey for horticultural trade. With as many as five million *Cyclamen* corms collected in Turkey in a single year, it is little wonder that certain species have been driven to the brink of extinction in the wild. The problem was compounded by the requirement that the bulbs be collected whilst in flower. As this is the most vulnerable time for bulbs, losses were higher than necessary and no seed was set. The village people who did the collecting had to travel further and further to find the plants, for which they were paid very little. And there were fewer and fewer plants to find. This time, *C. mirabile* really was on the brink of extinction in the wild. *Sternbergia candida* (autumn crocus) was another species whose over-collection at this time threatened its survival in its own home. The wild occurrence of *Aloe suzanne*, a dramatic succulent from Madagascar, has also suffered from both habitat destruction and collection for the horticultural trade.

The disappearance of species from the wild in this way is a concern for ecological and economic reasons. Ecologically, the removal of any species, plant or animal, from an ecosystem has reverberations that echo throughout that system. The loss of a single nut of seemingly minimal importance from an aeroplane could ultimately lead to its crashing, as vibrations spread from that unstable point, affecting more and more of the plane's structure, compounding the problem. The same is true within nature's systems. While we purchase cyclamen or autumn crocus for the delicate beauty they bring to our lives, much as we would purchase an ornament, in their natural habitat they have a practical role to play, and other life forms in that habitat rely on them being there, just as the whole plane relies on each single nut and bolt being in place and secure. Biologically, each element within a system is connected with other elements, as food, shelter, for breeding purposes or other more subtle functions. The Fauna and Flora International website states: 'Hillsides in Turkey once covered in wild flowers are now desolate as a result of this international trade in wild bulbs. Buying wild-collected bulbs for your garden threatens the very existence of these flower species in their natural habitat.'[5]

In the human economy, those village people who collect the bulbs and corms also lead precarious lives. Paid as little as a few dollars per 1000 bulbs, over-collection means loss of even this meagre livelihood. The plants have been mined, and mines have a limited life. When the mined product is gone, the ghost town remains. Fortunately for the people of Turkey, the alarm was raised. Controls and quotas have been introduced and propagation projects initiated by Fauna and Flora International. The cultivation of bulbs is a win-win activity. The village people are developing a sustainable industry and no longer have to clamber miles across the Anatolian hillsides in search of rarer and rarer flowers. The first cultivated bulbs from the Indigenous Propagation Project were harvested in May 1996. Gardeners in the West also gain, as higher quality, correctly identified bulbs are produced in cultivation. Labelling regulations have also been tightened up in Holland, so that wild-harvested bulbs must be labelled accordingly. The export of *Cyclamen mirabile* from Turkey is now illegal. The dangers of over-collection are being publicised and a national bulb collection has been established to ensure the preservation of rare species and the availability of propagation material.

However, gardeners still need to educate themselves and be vigilant when buying bulbs, especially in this era of internet sales. Countries other than Holland do not necessarily have responsible labelling regulations. In countries other than Turkey, wild-bulb harvest has not attracted so much attention and quotas and propagation projects are unlikely to exist. For example, farmers in Hungary and former Soviet states such as Georgia dig snowdrops for sale to Dutch exporters. The extent and impact of this practice is not known. Gardeners should beware of very cheap bulbs and bulbs of small and variable sizes, as these are likely to be wild harvested.

Closer to home for Australians is the national and international trade in some of our own highly sought-after, unusual-looking, slow-growing, long-lived plants that are often wild-harvested. These include species from the genera *Cyathea* and *Dicksonia* (the tree ferns); *Cycas*, *Lepidozamia* and *Macrozamia* (the cycads); *Livistona* (fan palm); *Lycopodium* (clubmoss); and *Xanthorrhoea* (grass tree). *Dicksonia antarctica*, cut largely from the holocaust sites of forestry clear-fells in Tasmania and Victoria, is exported in its hundreds of thousands, particularly to the UK, where trendy garden makeover programs can't get enough of its instant, lush good looks. The UK imported 140 000 tree ferns between 1996 and 2000. During this time an average of 12 ferns per day were seized as illegal imports.

The cutting of tree ferns in Tasmania follows the wholesale clearing of the forests in which they grow. They are a by-product of the woodchip, and to a lesser extent, timber industries which pay scant regard to the inadequate provisions that exist for the protection of water courses and endangered species such as the Tasmanian wedge-tailed eagle, let alone the ecology as a whole. These days the chief target species for old-growth logging are not rainforest species, but the eucalypts that grow in the mixed forest that is in transition towards becoming climax rainforest. Majestic gum trees — including the species which boasts the tallest-known trees ever to have grown on this Earth — grow side-by-side with the vivid greens of rainforest plants. The tallest tree ever was a *Eucalyptus regnans*, the king of the gum trees, and it grew in Victoria where it was measured at 132.6 metres after felling, and is believed to have originally been more than 150 metres tall. Today, the second tallest trees known to grow on this planet stand in small islands of reserve, surrounded by the devastation of clear-fell in the Styx Valley on the edge of Tasmania's famous South-West World Heritage area. By small, I mean maybe 10 hectares.

In the understorey of these once great forests grow an abundance of soft tree ferns, *Dicksonia antarctica*. In Tasmania, the trunks are used to make bush tracks or sold to gardeners for as little as A\$3 per foot (30 cm). It is obviously more lucrative to enter the international trade: in the UK, they fetch around £35 per foot, adding up to hundreds of pounds for the taller ferns. Australian export laws require a licensing system for individual specimens. This does not exist in Tasmania, so they are shipped to Victoria, and sold on from there.

In 1997 the Biodiversity Group of Environment Australia (a Federal Government department) commissioned a report into the domestic trade in wild-harvested long-lived native plants. The research involved a telephone survey of 291 native plant sellers, with the following findings:

135 sold wild harvested native plants. Interviewers reported that many respondents did not know whether the plants that they sold were wild harvested or artificially propagated. For some species the smaller plants in pots tended to be artificially propagated while the larger plants tended to be wild harvested. In the Queensland interviews, there was evident reluctance to provide information on wild harvested plant sales. Interviewers concluded that this might have related to prevalence of illegal harvesting. Overall, 12% of respondents reported that they had been offered illegally harvested plants.[6]

After *Dicksonia,* the grass tree *Xanthorrhoea australis* is sold in the next greatest numbers. Australian gardeners should take great care to check that plants from the above-mentioned groups have been propagated for sale, or second-best, legally harvested.

The USA has its own homegrown wild-harvest problems. The most obvious is the illegal trade in cacti from Mexico, within whose borders lie 85 percent of the biologically rich Chihuahuan Desert. Many of these plants are 'laundered' through Texas, so that it looks as though they have been permit-collected. Again, there are the two markets — the obsessive collectors keen for the rarest and strangest, and the gardeners and landscapers looking for instant effect. The trend to low-water gardening, known as xeriscaping, is a positive one in terms of water use. However, feeding the demand for plants in this style of garden has created a multimillion dollar industry in which illegal harvesting and trade of cacti and succulents is rife.

On 20th January 2003, *Prickly Trade: trade and conservation of Chihuahuan Desert Cacti* was released by TRAFFIC, the wildlife trade monitoring network of the World Wildlife Fund (WWF) and the World Conservation Union (IUCN). It stated, 'Unsustainable trade could endanger certain populations of cacti if measures are not taken to regulate their harvesting. The Chihuahuan Desert is home to almost a quarter of the 1,500 cactus species known to science, including many species found nowhere else on Earth.'

Although deserts look bare and simple, the very harshness of the conditions can lead to astonishing adaptive ingenuity and diversity of life forms. The isolation caused by the adverse conditions can also foster uniqueness, resulting in high percentages of species found nowhere else. This is so in the Chihuahuan Desert, where a patchwork of habitats supports one of the richest desert ecosystems in the world, surpassed only by the Namib-Karoo of southern Africa and the Great Sandy Desert of Australia. Remarkably, the report tells us that in the Chihuahuan Desert there are 'more mammal species than the Greater Yellowstone ecosystem, more bird species than the Florida Everglades, more plant species than the forests of the Pacific Northwest, and more reptile species than the Sonoran Desert'.[8] Also surprisingly, the list of species found nowhere else contains not only reptiles and plants, but also fish. As we know, the interactions between plants and other life forms can be very specific and interdependent. Take away plants, and you also take away wildlife.

Christopher Robbins, a botanist with TRAFFIC and co-author of the report describes the situation bluntly:

> *If we don't reduce the demand for wild plants, especially cacti, from the Chihuahuan Desert, we run the risk of jeopardizing populations and losing species. A whole range of desert dwellers — from hummingbirds to mountain lions — rely on desert plants for food or shelter. So in some situations, removing the cactus can be as disruptive to the ecosystem as clear-cutting a forest.*[9]

The demand for cacti from the Chihuahuan Desert is international. Although the USA is the largest market, England, Germany, Sweden,

Spain, Mexico, Italy and Canada, in that order, are all significant players in this trade.

There is no rest for ever-vigilant conservationists whose caring must constantly be converted into creative, inclusive solutions if their aims are to be effective. As with the bulb propagation projects in Turkey, non-government organisations have stepped in to help set up community-based nurseries growing desert plants. The WWF is initiating such programs, which also aim to develop nature-based tourism in west Texas, an area of high unemployment, as well as ecological richness.

These thoughtful programs tend to be multi-faceted, encompassing the social and economic factors involved as well as the environmental ones. It is interesting to note that in his book *Good News for a Change*, David Suzuki contends that when business takes environmental care as its starting point, rather than the economic bottom line, not only is there financial success, but social benefits also flow.

Of course, there is another risk associated with spreading hardy plants around the globe in this market-driven way. Away from the checks and balances of their own environment, weediness is a real possibility. Australia need look no further than its desperate experience of the prickly pear, a cactus that took over vast areas of arid and semi-arid country in the early 20th century. Fortunately, long-term biological control was achieved with the help of another import, the Cactoblastis moth, a 'pest' of the prickly pear.

Before moving on from the involvement of gardeners in species depletion in the wild, there is one more odd plant whose discovery has set in train a whole tactical exercise based around its stable, but tiny wild population. Back in Australia, it is worth taking a quick look at this strange plant, and the strategy in place to protect its stable, but tiny wild population. It is a botanical curiosity, and its peaceful and secret home is the rugged and enigmatic wilderness beyond the tentacles of Sydney's seemingly endless urban expansion.

A tree, now named the Wollemi pine *Wollemia nobilis*, was known only as a fossil until 1994. In this year a stand was discovered in an isolated canyon in a national park northwest of Sydney. To date, less than 100 trees have been counted in three locations. Fossil records tell us that the species has been on Earth for 90–100 million years. The sites have been kept top secret, as the greatest threats to the survival in the wild of this no-longer extinct grandfather of the tree world are disease (such as the root rot, *Phytophthora cinnamomi*) carried in on the boots of the curious, vandalism, fire and poaching.

An ambitious propagation and marketing program is under way to ensure that the Wollemi pine does not become extinct and the species is made so widely available that poaching will be discouraged. Millions of the plants are due for international commercial release in 2005–6. This world loves gimmickry, and the Wollemi pine has all the attributes for commercial success in such a world. Those who wish to conserve not only the Wollemi pine, but other rare and endangered species and ecosystems, are using the commercial potential of the 'living fossil' to raise much needed money for plant conservation in Australia.

As you walk in your own garden, so familiar to you in all its nooks, crannies, beauty and idiosyncrasies, these thoughts of strange and exotic plants disappearing from their native habitats may seem distant and best left for someone else to think about. The rate of plant extinction, however, is an alarming figure that most people, including gardeners, are unaware of. It is estimated that one in 10 known plant species are now either rare or endangered. When you consider that species extinction is like a snowball gathering in size and momentum as it rolls, the implications of what is happening start to become clear. The interaction and interdependence of living things means that each loss or diminishing population affects other life forms, which are connected to other life forms, which are connected to other life forms, and on it goes, interminably, like links and jewels falling off a chain and out of a chain, until all that remains are weak and isolated sections, increasingly simple and dull and vulnerable.

These are the remnants of natural areas, with which we are already so familiar that they seem normal. These include the bits of urban bushland strangled by exotic vines and cut through with stormwater drains and messed up with bits of plastic and broken glass, that some earnest people, often gardeners, spend their precious weekends trying to restore and maintain. These places never needed the hand of gardeners in the past. They were independent and involved no dollar economy or strategic thinking to survive. All that has changed — and it is the values of humans that have changed it. We are the top consumer in that chain, and to the best of our knowledge, the only ones conscious of their actions — but with consciousness comes responsibility and power.

Gardeners have a role to play in this, within their own backyards, as well as helpers in nature conservation. This is why gardeners who accept their responsibility and the power of their actions need to think beyond organics, and be informed of issues such as wild-plant harvest and its implications, so that when they chance upon a new cactus or bulb or orchid or something else interesting and 'novel', they know to be vigilant and check its pedigree. Otherwise, you participate in the demise of our planet's treasure chest of life, not a speck of which has been detected in any of the other galaxies or universes that our cleverness has enabled us to spy on.

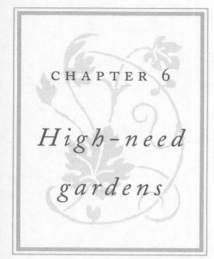

CHAPTER 6

High-need gardens

LOW-MAINTENANCE GARDENING HAS BECOME a popular idea. Time is precious, and many people feel unskilled in the garden. The Anglo/European gardening styles that Australia inherited have their origins in faraway lands with gentle summers, soft, regular rains and deep soils that have been carefully tilled for 1000 or more years. This type of garden and its plants are hard work in Australia, especially when the work has to be done under the heat of an intense and glaring sun, in the drenching humidity of coastal summers from Sydney to the far north, or braced against the cold or hot winds that blow off ocean, mountains and desert.

This is particularly true of gardens based around lawns, annual flower beds and roses, as well as for fruit and vegetables. These and other 'hard-to-grow' plants require regular and heavy inputs of fertiliser, water and pest and disease control sprays to keep them looking good. High-need plants are those that depend the most on the gardener for their health and success. Which ones they are varies according to regional soil and climate conditions. So, the enticingly labelled 'low-maintenance gardening', could perhaps be more correctly termed 'appropriate' or 'commonsense' gardening. In other words, it's all relative. If ordinary gardening is by implication 'high-maintenance', that is largely because it is inappropriate to the environment in which it exists.

However, the low-maintenance idea is not always so important to people who *enjoy* gardening. These people are curious, idealistic and often thrive on the challenge of growing that which is 'hard to grow' or different. They have skills; they are craftspeople and artists in their gardens, and also find deep joy in the experience of exploring the plant world in this way. Other people who want a certain 'look' are prepared to work extra hard to achieve it, or pay others to make their vision a reality. And then there are those who rely on advice from salespeople and the plethora of English/global gardening publications that are cover-to-cover with inspiration and clever photography of desirable flowers and green lawns, but very short on knowledge of local growing conditions for your part of Australia. Often the gorgeous, colourful gardens of books and magazines are made up of high-need plants—high-need, that is, in most Australian conditions. These gardens and plants are never promoted as being 'high-maintenance', in the way that 'low-maintenance' is used as a selling point.

The disastrous consequences of using modern poisons in farming and gardening have been well documented, from the 1962 publication of Rachel Carson's *Silent Spring* to the present day. The detrimental effects of many modern fertilisers to soil ecology are well known. I am assuming that most readers already avoid the use of what I call 'modern' poisons and fertilisers in the garden. These are the agricultural and gardening chemicals that have in the main become widely available post-World War II. What largely concerns us here are gardening practices which seem innocent, but which may in fact be contributing to the negative impact of gardens in the ecological big picture. The idea is to maximise the positive role of gardens in the environment. In order to do that, it is vital to be aware of the negatives, however subtle they may be. The area of high-need plant, therefore, needs a close look.

The organic gardening movement has attempted to address the problems resulting from the struggle with nature that is so often a part of gardening. In response to concerns about the negative environmental impacts of gardening practices, there are now a multitude of 'natural' and 'organic' fertilisers and sprays on the market, as well as information on how to make your own and how to use water efficiently. These are a step in the right direction, yes. However, the ecological impact is still greater than if these inputs were not required at all. Nutrient run-off occurs from manures and composts as well as from synthesised fertilisers. Algal blooms and increased weed growth along drainage lines and water courses are encouraged just the same. Many natural- or plant-based sprays are broad-spectrum poisons, or have deterrent effects which can also influence the beneficial insects, interrupting the development of a balance that will keep pests in check without the gardener needing to spend money or do work.

This summer as I have been writing, I take occasional breaks from my desk to visit a favourite peach tree. The tree suffered badly from leaf curl (a fungus) last year, and so I sprayed once with bordeaux before bud burst. Hardly any fruit has set, as the tree was in bad shape at the time of bud formation last autumn. However, this year it has a mighty crop of bright green leaves, it is building its reserves and I suspect will fruit well next time. With minimal leaf curl, but lots of sweet young growth, the aphids arrived to sip on the gently flowing sap, and the new growth started to deform. However, I did not interfere, though I could have gone in with pyrethrum or simply with a jet of water from the hose to remove the aphids. I knew from experience that both these measures bring only temporary respite and must be repeated again and again. I decided to wait, and observe nature taking its course. Soon, there were a couple of ladybirds and their strange-looking larvae on my observation branch. Next time I checked, I counted eight ladybirds on that one small twig! Now, both aphids and ladybirds have gone. All I have done is watch and admire and learn. *That* is low-maintenance, ecological gardening. It requires an understanding and a patience that leads to minimum intervention, rather than a *reactive* approach.

'Natural' fungicides should also be used conservatively. Copper-based fungal controls, such as the classic bordeaux mixture used on my peach, make their way into the soil, where repeated use can result in copper build-up over time. Copper is not needed in large quantities by plants. It is a micronutrient and copper toxicity can occur. And don't forget that the soil is alive too — with myriad bacteria and fungi. The majority of these fungi are beneficial to gardeners, and their vitality helps keep unwanted fungi such as root rots in check.

For example, the destructive root rot *Phytophora cinnamomi* can decimate avocado trees. Over the last two to three decades avocado trees have been planted in amongst banana plantations in some areas as a high-value, less labour-intensive crop that could ultimately replace the bananas. It has been noticed that these avocado trees thrive in this environment, where the felled banana trees provide mulch on the hot, steep slopes. When the bananas are cleared away, however, as the conversion to avocado production takes place, the trees begin to ail. The problem is phytphthora root rot. The solution, apart from soil drenches, is heavy mulching to maintain a soil high in organic matter and nitrogen, both of which encourage competitive, harmless fungi that discourage the rot. A healthy, living soil looks after its plants in many ways.

The usefulness of soil moulds and fungi is multidimensional. As most people know, they help with the decay of all that once lived. This is the cycling of organic matter that maintains soil structure and nutrient levels. As we shall read more of soon, there are also fungi that live with plant roots and help them extract otherwise inaccessible food from the soil. What effect does the dripping of 'safe' and 'natural' fungicides from the leaf canopy have on soil fungi? Ditto the dripping of natural insecticides into the soil zone, where worms and slaters and ants and crickets and tiny parasitic wasps and beetles and so many other miniature life forms go about their business? The soil ecology is a hidden and easily overlooked dimension in garden health. The best approach for those of us who have limited knowledge of the implications of our actions is to follow the advice of Hippocrates—*first, do no harm*.

AUSTRALIA'S NATURAL ABUNDANCE

Fertilising the common range of garden plants in Australia's 'low-nutrient' soils is a constant job for gardeners. Before looking at some of the problematic effects of fertilising, let's think again about our soils.

Generally, Australia is said to have 'poor' soils. This poverty refers to nutrient content and the ability of the soil to hold food and water in a form available to plants. This so-called poverty of the soil, however, is relative. Australia's so-called poor soils support some of the world's most biologically diverse and rich ecologies. The many, many thousands of plants that have evolved on this island continent have had all their needs met by these supposedly poor soils and in these supposedly harsh conditions for aeons. The diversity of Australia's floral species is remarkable. There are 1000-odd eucalypt species and about 600 acacias, to name only the most common of our genera. Australian plants have many adaptations that enable them to live perfectly well without any additional food, water or pest control. For example, the family Proteaceae (e.g. banksias, waratahs) have 'proteoid' roots— these are masses of very fine hair roots, whose abundance increases the surface area of the feeder roots giving much greater access to the soil and hence greater access to nutrients. The Proteaceae also have mychorrizal associations, which means that particular types of fungi exist in their root systems. The fungi act on soil nutrients in a way that makes otherwise inaccessible nutrients available to the plant.

The 'poor soil and harsh conditions' judgement was given to Australia by the English, whose cool-climate fruits, vegetables, soft lawns, sweet-flowered roses and broad-leaved trees suffered seriously from homesickness in much of this new land. It is a mindset we have adopted without critical thinking or appreciation of the Australian environment. It is also a mindset that forgets how many imported plants have run amok in Australia. Plants that behaved well in England— pretty garden shrubs like lantana, handsome trees like the camphor laurel, and useful hedging species such as privet don't find Australian soils 'poor', or conditions 'harsh'. No, they are quite happy with our soil conditions and also love to bask in the bright sunshine and drink deeply the warm water of subtropical downpours. They have no argument with our abundant bird life spreading their seeds far and wide. In fact, they seem to have no complaints at all, as they invade rolling pasture land, sheltered gullies and river banks in the mild climes of Australia's east coast.

The point is that many plants, both native and exotic, thrive in Australia without needing constant and heavy additions of fertiliser, water and sprays. And most exotics that fall into this group do not become weeds. We can have handsome and varied gardens with minimal inputs.

The work of an innovative and environmentally conscious landscape gardener in Sydney is worth a look at in this context. Andrew O'Sullivan's passion for using salvaged materials to build stylish gardens involves the use of salvaged plants. His salvage yard includes a nursery which is more aptly described as a rehab zone for maltreated plants. His habit of saving and reviving plants from demolition sites has, by default, created gardens that are ideally suited to Sydney's growing conditions. The gardens are also low-maintenance, simply because the plants are happy. Andrew says, 'The plant material I save is old, tough, hardy, reliable stuff that doesn't need fertilisers and sprays and water. It has proved its worth. These are the plants that do well in Sydney. When I save them, they are a bit rough round the edges, but with some TLC, they soon look rich and lush.' His use of these plants gives his gardens a subtropical feel, which earned them the label 'Balinese'. Plants like gingers, frangipani, tree ferns, palms, agaves and strelitzia thrive in Sydney's climate and soils. The gardening paradigm, or mindset, that is entrenched in our culture would say that these plants survive on neglect. Looked at from another angle, the viewpoint would be that they are appropriate to the environment, a quality which endows them with independence.

Gardens based around plants that are environmentally appropriate give to us in many ways — they need less work, so we have more time to enjoy them; they cost less money, so that they can be used in other ways; and they interact positively with the ecology beyond the fence line, particularly if planting and design are organised to maximise food and shelter for birds, insects, lizards, frogs and even small native mammals if we live near bushland.

By contrast, plants that need fertilising, watering and protection from pests have a negative environmental impact even if organic solutions are used. Often we are unaware of these effects because they occur beyond our fence lines, out of sight and out of mind. A Sydney resident with a keen interest in nature conservation wrote to me with his anecdotal observations of the 'effects of the fertilising that goes on in European-style gardens' which can be seen 'very dramatically' in some areas of northern Sydney, where homes and gardens sit on top of a plateau above the Lane Cove River. 'Spectacular plumes of green weeds cascade down into the creeks and valleys from the gardens above,' the concerned resident writes, 'but in road cuttings where there is no garden above, the bush is intact on the upside with almost no weeds.'

This anecdote is backed by studies that show a direct connection between high nutrient levels (especially of phosphorous) in run-off zones and weed growth in the bush. Phosphorous is the most problematic, as it moves slowly through the environment, accumulating in a way that the other major nutrients, nitrogen and potassium, don't. Many human activities add phosphorus to the environment. Robin Buchanan, in her excellent book *Bush Regeneration: recovering Australian landscapes*, explains what happens:

Where does the phosphorus come from? In an agricultural system it derives from superphosphate. In the urban scene ... it comes from washing powders, fertilisers, septic effluent, sewerage overflow, and most importantly domestic pets ...

Concentrations of phosphorus are about 50–100 times greater in urban stormwater than in waters in natural catchments in Sydney. Soil concentrations can be 10–20 times higher in areas affected by run-off.[1]

Soils below suburban boundaries, roads and stormwater outlets have significantly higher levels of phosphorus than comparable soils in the same locality. Invasive environmental weeds such as camphor laurel, privet, tradescantia and lantana thrive in these phosphorus-fed environments. Nutrients added to the garden in our quest to grow high-need plants from parts of the world with naturally rich soils, leach and seep down through the soil water and beyond the garden fence. Whether the fertiliser is natural or manufactured, it contributes to weed growth in both bushland and in waterways.

WATER WORRIES

Water in Australia is tricky. As a nation we seem to lurch from devastating drought to overwhelming flood. The droughts go on and on, year after year, each one seeming to be reported by the media as the worst in history. At least, that is the impression in my memory after living here for four decades, and it is on this type of impression that most people base their viewpoint. The fear and uncertainty surrounding climate change have added a new dimension of seriousness to extreme weather events globally. The incentive to manage our precious water resource is stronger than ever before. Australia is the driest continent, but the problem is global, and as demonstrated so graphically by the destructive wild harvesting of cacti and succulents to feed the low-water gardening trend in the US, many gardeners are trying to do the right thing in terms of water use.

Severe drought coupled with urban sprawl and water-use habits have strained the water-supply infrastructure of most Australian towns and cities in the last decade. Summer water restrictions have often become the norm, even when the dams are full, as a preventative measure, *just in case*. User-pays water metering is another strong incentive to change garden styles from green lawns and flower beds to hard landscaping such as paving, and hardier plants such as succulents and native species.

There is another reason, however, for gardeners to change their water-using ways. This reason lacks the drama and newsworthiness of drought, which comes neatly packaged with images of dying stock and distressed farmers walking off the land their family has worked for generations. This other issue is a major rural problem, and an emerging urban problem. It is not caused by the weather; it is caused by us, by people. I am talking about soil salinity.

Salinity is not usually associated with suburbia. It is considered a problem of farming, not gardening. Yet how many Australians realise that salinity affects a significant number of our towns and small cities, as well as the steadily expanding urban sprawls such as those of western Sydney?

While the crippling desiccation of drought reminds us that without water there is no life, salinity is caused by too much water in the wrong place. It is caused by an imbalance in the distribution of our water resource as a result of land-management practices, whether agricultural or urban. Soil salinity occurs when the water table rises, bringing with it a concentration of dissolved salts from deep down in the subsoils.

Obviously, waterlogging is another problem that comes with a high water table.

Why does the water table rise? It is quite simple. To start with, places that have a heavy clay soil or subsoil which inhibits drainage *and* a narrow point of groundwater discharge are most susceptible. These conditions make drainage naturally slow. When this land is cleared for farming or development, the vegetation that acted as a water pump, constantly transferring ground water into the atmosphere via transpiration is removed. Next, increasing amounts of water are added to irrigate crops or gardens. The suburban gardens and public recreation areas that replace the bush are largely based around shallow-rooting plants such as grasses, annual flowers and shrubs. Watering practices may also encourage shallow root systems, whereas the vegetation of the natural bush had to put down deep, searching roots if it was to survive seasons of low rainfall and extended drought. In suburbia, soil waterlogging and salinity cause expensive damage to roads, buildings and gas and water pipes as well as destroying gardens.

Recognition of this problem is changing the face of some Australian towns. Wagga Wagga, in south-western NSW, has led the way in researching how to manage this problem. Engineering solutions are complemented by complete makeovers of public plantings and nature strips. The high-need lawns and bedding plants are being replaced with mulched gardens of groundcovers and low shrubs which can survive the saline conditions and have minimal water needs. Long-term cost-savings in maintenance are significant, as these new gardens need neither mowing nor watering.

The repercussions of growing high-need plants are many and often subtle. As we have seen, high water inputs, along with vegetation removal, are causing salinity in the suburbs, not just on far-away irrigation farms. Plant-derived poisons are still poisons, and are often used with limited understanding of the range of insects they affect. Nutrient run-off from composts and manures can still encourage weed growth in the bush and algal bloom in our waterways. *Chapter 14— Growing high-need plants ecologically* looks at an ecological approach to growing some high-need plants. Fruit and vegetables come into that category. Home food production is an important part of environmentally positive gardening, due not only to the appalling way most food is grown and the energy requirements of packaging and transportation, but also the superior quality of flavour and nutrition in much homegrown food.

NEATNESS AND MINIMALISM IN GARDENS

Garden design fashions come and go. In the late 20th and early years of the 21st centuries, a trend towards minimalism has developed in garden design. Hard surfaces, few species and simple, clean lines and styling create an up-market garden that is effectively an ecological desert. These 'architectural' gardens are based purely around a human aesthetic. Aside from this ultra-simple garden aesthetic, extreme garden neatness in any garden style means less habitat and less positive interaction with the birds and the bees and the wider environment.

Writing on 'Nature in the Urban Garden', in the essay collection *The Meaning of Gardens*, Kerry J. Dawson observes:

> *The garden is too often an artificial world made up of disjunct*
> *natural objects where a high value is placed on order, efficiency,*

cleanliness, and segregation … Nature has its own architecture, one far more complicated and diverse than human architecture. The architecture of nature is ecology. Garden ecology is the application of this to gardens … The geometry of nature is therefore different from that of garden architecture both visually and structurally. People generally favour one layer of simplified, neat plantings, that produce an expansive visual effect … Forest bird species generally prefer layered clumps of vegetation instead of linear bands.[2]

These neat, highly controlled gardens are not friendly places for non-human creatures. Their gardeners are also more likely to use herbicides, including residual pre-emergent herbicides to help keep the clean look constant. The pre-emergents are commonly used in gravel driveways and on paths and edge areas where annoying little weeds tend to make quick headway when our backs are turned. They are also part of the lawn maintenance routine for those desirous of a pure green carpet but understandably unimpressed by the tedious task of weeding that carpet. These poisons rely on remaining toxic for a long time, generally around three months. They are applied directly to the ground, where run-off and seepage are likely, and their job is to literally nip life in the bud.

Remember that below the ground it is not a static world. Water flows, insects burrow and soil is relocated. The chemistry of the soil is complex and dynamic. How far do these herbicides travel, after application? Where do they go? What do they become when their chemical structure changes? While the gardener labours to maintain a fairly static look above ground, the soil, in the words of Rachel Carson in *Silent Spring*, 'exists in a state of constant change, taking part in cycles that have no beginning and no end.'[3] The changelessness we strive for is superficial, it is illusory, a denial even, and comes at a cost.

An article by Dr Kendra Baumgartner of the Department of Plant Pathology, University of California, raises the issue of groundwater contamination by the pre-emergent herbicides that contribute to the illusion of control: 'Pre-emergence herbicides have been found to contaminate both surface and ground waters due to their persistence in the soil. Growing concerns over water quality and impending legislation may make some pre-emergence herbicides unavailable. Alternatives may soon be a necessity.'[4]

Multidimensional gardens tend to be the most biologically rich. Nature loves layers. It loves to stack things one on top of the other, to make use of every available bit of space, from below ground to the tops of the highest trees. Every layer has its own ecology, from the dark underworld of soils, to the mulch of decaying leaf litter, the ground-covering plants, clumpers, herbs, shrubs small and large, trees small and large, as well as rocks, rotting logs and other paraphernalia that lie and fly around this world. A garden with an old forgotten wood heap or pile of rocks in the corner, messy places that no-one pays attention to, where 'weeds' flower and die, grasses grow long and brown, an old container catches rainwater, things are muddled up—these corners will be alive with activity, abuzz with comings and goings, dynamics of give and take, action. Compared with minimalist gardens or the clinical, neatly trimmed edges and softness of over-fed and watered lawns that have been sprayed with herbicides for weeds, fungicides for diseases, insecticides for grubs and beetles and possibly even poisons to kill worms (they make an annoying mess on the surface with their castings), these messy places are cradles of life.

In 1991 the Bird Observers Club of Australia (BOCA) conducted a Garden Birds Survey to help find out how the design and composition of our gardens affect bird diversity. The survey was based on 350 gardens. These were divided into three categories and the numbers of bird species regularly present were recorded. The results showed:

• Suburban lawn with trees and shrubs—18 bird species.

• Garden at the edge of woodland or park—27 bird species.

• Garden in woodland style with more or less continuous tree cover—30 bird species.[5]

The BOCA also looked in more detail at the role of tall trees and thick understorey in gardens. They found that an upper storey of tall indigenous trees, such as flowering gums, was very important for bringing a variety of birds. Additionally, some thick cover from treetops to ground level is essential for the survival of *small* birds. They need hiding places where they can safely feed and sleep. This type of continuous density is rare in suburbia. It is a structural aspect of planting design that must be given greater attention by gardeners if small bird populations are to have a chance in our towns, cities and farms. The well-ordered garden where a lawn is dotted or edged with flowerbeds, trimmed shrubs and perhaps a feature tree offers little security for the nervous, sharp-eyed birds whose sometimes tiny size gives them no ability to defend themselves or their territory against the aggression of larger birds, cats, dogs and people. Dense, preferably prickly shrubberies are a must in the bird-friendly garden. Gardeners generally avoid prickly trees and shrubs, and design-conscious gardeners often prefer a so-called 'sculptural' or minimalist look to the more overgrown, casual effect of thick, continuous vegetation. Through our self-obsession, we exclude nature.

It is only when we try to see gardening from nature's point of view that we are able to bring together gardening values and nature conservation values in a comprehensive way. We can do this by incorporating the technical know-how of organic gardeners, a basic scientific understanding of the micro-ecosystems that combine to form the garden ecosystem and their relationship to the wider ecology, and a wisdom which understands the living world as a web in which each strand is ultimately linked, and in which each act and action has repercussions, whether we are aware of them or not. Thinking about gardening from nature's point of view also enables us to take an honest look at the negative effects of many standard gardening practices, which at face value may seem harmless.

PART 3

The evolution

of modern

organic

gardening

The interconnectedness of all things on Earth means
that everything we do has consequences that
reverberate through the systems of which we are a part.
When we reclaim this ancient understanding,
we will recover the sense of responsibility that it entails.

David Suzuki, *The Sacred Balance*

CHAPTER 7

The early days

ORGANIC GARDENING HAS EXISTED FOR AS LONG AS gardens have been made. However, from the time that science started dabbling in soil fertility and the management of crop pests and diseases, there arose what is now referred to as 'conventional' farming and gardening methods. These 'conventional' methods largely rely on factory-produced chemicals to fix plant health problems. It was in the post–World War II period that the use of these chemicals went berserk, the scale of their use far outstripping our fledgling understanding of their sinister nature, and of the ecologies into which we poured them. From the 1940s through to the 1970s in particular, some of the most lethal poisons ever known were used with little care and much bravado, being *aerial sprayed* over vast tracts of land, especially in the USA. Taxpayer-funded spray programs intended to 'eradicate' individual species of beetles or flies that were perceived as a nuisance or potential threat, no doubt made a few industrialists wealthy, but they did not eradicate the beetles or flies, and left a legacy of ecological horror.

In those not-so-far-off days, every hygienic Western household had aerosol cans of deadly poison in the cupboard, often the kitchen cupboard, for targeting the odd fly, mosquito, cockroach or spider that buzzed or crept uninvited within the walls of the home. And if you had a garden, you had garden chemicals in the cupboard as well.

In our house there was a dark brown bottle of 2-4D on the high shelf in the hall cupboard. As I recall, it was labelled 'Brush and Blackberry

Killer'. My parents were environmentalists before most people had thought about it, but every so often the brown bottle would come out of hiding as Dad donned overalls, boots and rubber gloves in a weekend bid to 'control' the blackberry bushes that grew down the back. 'Down the back' was a rough, damp track that led to a coastal lagoon. I learned to swim in that lagoon, messed around catching small fish in submerged milk bottles and felt the weird, oozy squish of mud between my small toes. Then in the early 1970s the signs went up. This lagoon is polluted. Swim at your own risk. Dad was not the only one using residual chemicals in the lagoon's catchment area. Not far upstream were a golf course and other playing fields.

The art of greenkeeping involves making large areas of monocultural grass short and smooth and green by killing or preventing the occurrence of all life forms that compromise this in any way and adding as much nitrogen fertiliser as it takes to maintain the small green leaves which are constantly mown to within less than an inch of their tedious lives. Life forms which need killing in this scenario include insects, earthworms, fungi, bacteria and unwanted plants. Fish, ducks, aquatic insects, water plants and children learning to swim are not included directly, but neither are they excluded, as drainage lines and water tables don't differentiate between poisons in solution and poisons pure water.

I don't remember being alarmed by the *Don't Swim* signs. I was growing up in a world in which pollution was normal. I swam in the ocean instead, amongst the muck and debris from the sewerage plant that emptied from one of Sydney's most famous scenic headlands into the waters of one of Sydney's most famous scenic beaches. Occasionally signs went up on the sand to say that pollution was bad today, better not swim, but closing Manly Beach permanently to swimming was unthinkable. It would have been very bad for business, and also for politicians.

It was in these times, when the evidence of pollution and ecological crisis came into our own backyards and could not be ignored, that the organic farming and gardening 'movement' gathered momentum. The fallout from Carson's *Silent Spring* continued, as it must. In 1962 she had written:

> *Gardening is now linked with the super poisons. Every hardware store, garden-supply shop and supermarket has rows of insecticides, for every conceivable horticultural situation. Those who fail to make wide use of this array of lethal sprays and dusts are by implication remiss, for almost every newspaper's garden page and the majority of gardening magazines take their use for granted … Little is done, however, to warn the gardener or homeowner that he is handling extremely dangerous materials.*[1]

It is remarkable how quickly this chemical mindset had taken over, and shows the incredible level of trust that the general populace place in science, government and business. For the whole of human history we had managed without these things. All of a sudden, they seemed indispensable. Fifty years of mass communication and mass marketing later, we are perhaps more cynical, and hopefully a little wiser. But as I look back, I see that it has taken *repeated ecological crises* to fuel the development of the organic movement to the point where today it can be regarded as mainstream, rather than a 'movement'. Thankfully, organics is now becoming 'normal' and it must seem astonishing to new gardeners that this approach was ever regarded as oddball and fringe. After all, what kind of idiot would spend their leisure time applying deadly nerve poisons to their favourite roses, to the lawns they walk and play on, and to the fruit and vegetables they plan to eat? These are the same roses that they love to lean into and breath deeply of the fragrance, the same roses that they bring into the home as cut flowers to adorn the living areas peopled by loved ones and pets, the same lawns that they tread barefoot, and that children roll on and fall on as they run with their dog or their friend, the same fruit and vegetables that they proudly present as home grown. What kind of idiot would do such a thing?

Perhaps I was fortunate to be maturing in the 1970s, when there was both awareness and idealism to tap into. Perhaps I was fortunate to have at this time a passion for both wild nature and the domesticated nature of the garden. I feel that in a sense organic gardening and I have grown up together—that I started gardening according to the organics of the mid-1970s and have absorbed and delved into and watched the various trends and fads that have influenced it over the last 30 years. In this time there has been much change. Organic gardening has become more complex, more refined, more ambitious and more environmental. What follows is the story of that development, as *I* have perceived it. It is this development, this evolution of organics that enables us to now look at going beyond it and into environmental gardening.

THE RISE OF ORGANICS

The focus of organics, initially, was to promote substitutes for the organo-chlorine and organo-phosphate pesticides, and the pure-nutrient fertilisers that dominated the shelves of agricultural and gardening stores.

There was a solid base of knowledge that had been maintained through the dark ages of chemical madness by wise people who had kept their connection with the living soil and could see the link between human health and a natural, healthy environment. There were groups such as the UK-based The Soil Association (founded 1946) and the Henry Doubleday Research Association (founded 1954), and the US Rodale Institute (founded late 1940s), plus the groundswell of the alternative lifestyle movement, all of whom were there in the background as a resource, preserving and building on the knowledge base and positioned to start feeding the information out to the rest of us. These passionate people researched and wrote about companion planting, biological controls, composting, natural insecticides, mulching, natural soil management and other cultural and technical aspects of the science of gardening and farming without the use of synthesised or highly toxic products. The emphasis was on food production for personal and planetary health.

Compared with the bounty of literature now available on organics, however, there was precious little information available in those pre-internet days for a budding organic gardener like myself. In 1977, aged 16, I clearly remember searching the bookshops for *anything* on organic gardening. I came up with one English publication, *The Mother Earth Manual of Organic Gardening*, and one Australian booklet, written in Tasmania. They were all about vegetable growing, which I soon found out was not so easy where I lived. For one thing, where was I to get all the lucerne hay and manure, or any hay, straw or manure for that matter, which was apparently *essential* for success, and which access to seemed taken for granted by these manuals? I lived in the city, by the beach. My family were interested in sun and sand and good books, not hay and manure. Not to be put off, I seconded a bit of garden space amongst the trees and sandstone, added some compost to the gritty, grey soil, and grew a bed of happy-looking tomato plants. The great harvest day arrived. Every single tomato was crawling with teeny white maggots. Thus, I learned about fruit fly, an important insect pest not present in England or Tasmania, and therefore not mentioned in either of my organic gardening guides.

Four years later in 1981, as a horticulture student, I found that there was still very little Australian writing on horticulture in general, let alone organics. Even the first of the complex Permaculture books, which was out by then, was written from a base of Tasmanian experience. Like many Australians, I lived in Sydney, not England or Tassie. Soils of loose, grey sand; languid, humid days; wild, stormy deluges; no frosts; fruit fly everywhere; no need to know about codling moth, because I couldn't grow apples anyway. The books were full of information on frost protection, the need for full sun, and companion herbs that apparently repelled insects of a much more timid nature than those that thrived in my warm-temperate climate. Plus, in the northern hemisphere, the seasons are the wrong way round. It was all rather tedious to a young person with a great thirst for knowledge. I battled on, taking up with a boyfriend who taught me more about gardening in Sydney than the books did.

By the late 1980s, however, the tide had turned. Organic gardening tomes, both local and international, had found their place on bookstore shelves. By the information-obsessed 1990s, the trickle had turned to a flood, as organics became an industry in itself. This trend continues.

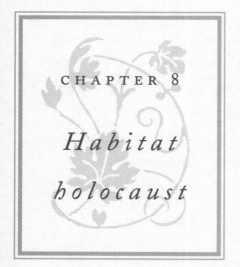

CHAPTER 8

Habitat holocaust

ALL THIS TIME I WAS LOOKING FOR INFORMATION on organics, the development of agribusiness was forging ahead in the West, as well as pushing into the so-called Third World. The chemicalisation of agriculture was only part of the story. Some other ecological lessons were about to be learned the hard way.

Ultimately, all roads seem to have led to Rome. The Rome of this story is the absolute need to look after global biodiversity if we are to maintain planetary health. By maintaining biodiversity, I mean maintaining life.

All life forms need homes. We call these homes habitats when the life form being discussed is not human. While the rain of pesticides targets individual life forms themselves, habitat destruction is equivalent to the bulldozing or burning down or the collapsing in an earthquake of entire suburbs or cities. Even if you are alive, having survived both the spraying and the disintegration, you have nowhere to go, and probably no food to eat. Habitat loss in rural environments showed us the importance of having complex ecosystems within our own living areas. For organic gardeners it was perhaps the catalyst for wanting to *attract* birds rather than repel them. All sorts of connections fell into place when we realised that birds and insects were friends of the garden rather than enemies. A bit later on, for other reasons which will be discussed, the frog pond became a must. But these elements seeped into the kit bag of organic gardening gradually, and only because of lessons learnt from habitat disasters in agricultural areas.

THE HEDGEROWS OF ENGLAND

Wherever there is a long history of agriculture and gardening, there you also find 'semi-natural' habitat. The woodlands and hedgerows of England are beautiful examples of these. They have been there so long, that although they are man-made and managed, nature has adapted to their presence, and a harmony, an equilibrium that characterises mature ecosystems, has arisen. This equilibrium depends on human involvement, for *Homo sapiens* is an important animal species in the matrix of these ecosystems. If the farmers cease to manage the hedgerows, they change, appearing 'neglected' as they begin the transformation into something else. Such neglect is definitely the better side of the coin in the story of hedgerow decline in the UK.

The hedgerows of England were fully established 2000 years ago when a frustrated Julius Caesar declared them impossible to penetrate. Their management is believed to date back 5000 years, to the agriculture of the Bronze Age farmers. These ancient hedgerows—in effect, long narrow forests—are whole ecologies in themselves, providing habitat for numerous species of birds, insects and plants, and preserving the ecology of another time. What is left, however, is much less than it was. The hunger of machines is insatiable. At the end of World War II, 800 000 km of hedgerows criss-crossed the UK. As agriculture modernised in the post-war era, the hedgerows seemed old and in the way. Machines were getting bigger, so fields needed to get bigger. Small fields mean a lot of turning around time for big machines. If you have been convinced that time is money, then small fields are an unnecessary expense and it makes sense to enlarge them. Small farms were becoming less common in any case, as amalgamations proceeded under agribusiness imperatives. And if you did need a divider to control stock or mark a boundary, fencing wire could be bought, and would not need trimming or coppicing. Shelter needed for lambing and calving, previously provided at no extra cost by the hedges, could be built. And all that messy habitat—surely it was a breeding ground for weeds, pests and diseases?

These and other apparently rational reasons for *not* having hedgerows seemed so important and true that at one stage farmers could actually claim a government subsidy for ripping them out. By the year 2000, less than half the hedgerows remained, and the government had changed its mind about what was in the nation's best interests. In 1989, following a decade of rampant removal, farmers became eligible for a subsidy to *plant and maintain* their hedge systems, and in 1998, the Hedgerow Regulations Bill was passed, making hedgerow removal without permission a criminal offence. Whichever way you look at it, after minding their own business and peacefully beautifying the countryside for 5000 years, hedgerows have cost the English taxpayer a lot of money in the last 25 years.

But what else was lost, besides taxpayers' money? Homes were lost — homes for countless life forms that have no say in the spending of tax dollars. Hedgerows are a key habitat for more than 60 bird species, including some who travel vast distances each year to nest and feed in their dynamic ecology. Whitethroats and blackcaps from Africa come for the summer, while in winter, redwings from Scandinavia take their place. Mammals including hedgehogs, moles, shrews, badgers and weasels live in hedgerows while bats feed on the numerous invertebrates that are part of these ecosystems. Farmland birds depend on these linear forests. Their numbers, particularly of grey partridges, song thrushes, linnets, bullfinches and corn buntings, have declined sharply with the demolition of their homes.

These intricate wildlife corridors were also windbreaks, creating a sheltered network of microclimates that increased the productivity of the farms. They protected soil from erosion by reducing wind strength, minimising water run-off and binding the soil with their deep, stable root complexes. Their involvement in groundwater systems must also have been considerable, as deep-rooting trees are like water pumps in the cycling of water, and the biomass of all plants, but particularly trees due to their bulk, are living water reservoirs. While the modern farmers with hygiene on their minds may have thought of hedgerows as hotbeds of pests, weeds and diseases lining their otherwise tidy farms, in fact the reverse was true. The hedgerows were homes to the natural predators of crop pests. As nesting sites for birds this was particularly so. Nestlings need a high-protein diet to fuel their fast growth while the season is warm. That means their busy parents make a lot of trips into the field to catch insects. These interactions between farm and hedgerow evolved together, depending on each other for stability and permanence.

As if the organised and subsidised destruction of rural habitats across England wasn't enough, in the early 1970s her beloved elm trees started dying without subsidy or government sanction. Elm trees were an integral and beautiful part of the hedgerows, as well as of the countryside in general. The dying of elm trees from a fungal infection named Dutch elm disease (DED) was epidemic by 1973, compounding the disastrous destruction of rural habitat that was underway for reasons of economic rationalism, and continuing the aggressive transformation and trampling of the gentle English countryside which had begun with the industrial revolution.

The loss of the hedgerows and elms was followed by a sharp rise in insect pests attacking the vast acreages of monocultural crops so beloved of agribusiness. The predators that had lived in the hedgerows were gone, and monocultures of hybridised food crops bred for high productivity under ideal conditions lay across the wide open countryside like feasts spread in readiness for insects whose rate of reproduction was limited only by the availability of food. The birds, the frogs, the predatory and parasitic insects and many other critters and micro-organisms unknown to me, whose homes had been in the quaint hedges and ditches, were dead. This diverse and undemanding team of helpers had been overlooked by those who, pardon the expression, could not see the forest for the trees.

Insect populations quickly develop resistance to sprays. Unless there is a 100 percent kill, the survivors live to breed another day. And breed they do, each generation giving rise to a greater number of spray-survivors. Soon, virtually the entire population is immune to the poisons. Industrial chemists are paid good money to come up with a new 'solution', actually a new poison, to 'protect' the high-value crops. These poisons rain down on the land, from the boom sprays of the giant machines that crush the once-soft soil, and from natty little planes that love those wide-open spaces provided by the bulldozing of the trees and hedgerows. It is all very expensive and important-feeling. The birds and frogs and ladybirds did what they did for free, but no-one seemed to notice. I guess they were just part of the scenery, and as their value in the ecological 'economy' did not show up on company financial statements, they were not perceived to *have* a value. Their value and role as pollinators is another thing for which boardroom decision-makers did not have a column.

The dramatic decline in populations of British farm birds — key predators in the rural ecology — since the mid-1970s reflects an overall biodiversity crisis. Bird populations are regarded as good indicators of the biodiversity of a region, as they are widely distributed and are high on the food chain. The destruction of hedgerows has only been one aspect of semi-natural rural habitat loss due to the intensification of agriculture in the UK. A large percentage of the traditional hay meadows, lowland heaths, ponds, woodlands, wetlands and grasslands that existed before World War II are now gone. The UK makes a good case study, as 70 percent of its land area is farmed, and as we have seen, the landscape has been shaped for so long by agriculture. As an industrialised nation it has been subjected to the full impact of modernisation. And as the world's leading gardening nation, it is from England that many gardening trends derive.

Concern is now widespread for the disappearing wildlife of England, and both organic farming and 'wildlife gardening' look set to play key roles in biodiversity recovery. More on that later. For now, more bad news from the 1970s and 1980s. This time, from the wide-acre properties of Australia where farm trees were dying for no obvious reason. Ironically, the area where this happened is called New England.

Eucalyptus die back in Australia

As old England was losing its hedgerows and elms, on the other side of the world, a mysterious form of dieback was decimating native tree stands in a farming area of north-western NSW known as New England. The once-beautiful properties of this lonely, remote landscape became tree graveyards dominated by the grey skeletons of dead eucalypts, the most important tree genus in Australia. No single disease or cause of death could be identified. It was concluded that a combination of factors had led to a weakening of the trees' resistance to attack by insects and disease.

These factors included: pasture improvement, resulting in optimal conditions for the breeding up of leaf-eating insects whose larval stage is in the soil; fertilising of these exotic pastures, which changed the chemical content of eucalypt leaves making them more palatable to defoliating and sap-sucking insects; soil compaction from overstocking with hard-hoofed animals (sheep and cattle), reducing the trees' overall health and weakening their ability to resist wood borers and other pests; secondary infections, which come in the form of wood rots that gain entry via the damage made by the borers; and loss of habitat for predatory birds and insects that help control leaf-attacking insects such as the Christmas beetle (happily breeding up on the roots of the rich pasture grasses) and gum-tree scale, which then gave these pests a free run. Basically, the trees died of stress-related illnesses. They were worn out by the battle to survive in an environment that now favoured their enemies.

Greening Australia is an organisation that was formed in 1982 to help reverse the trend of tree loss in human-managed landscapes. In a Greening Australia publication, *Birds on Farms: a New England perspective* (1993), authors Geoff Barrett and Hugh Ford of the University of New England observe that:

> *It is becoming clear that sustainable agriculture is dependent upon there being a healthy native ecosystem throughout the agricultural landscape ... Nowhere is this better illustrated than the pastoral landscape on the New England Tablelands, where eucalypt dieback is largely caused by leaf-eating insects. In areas where the native ecosystem is still intact dieback is less evident and there is good reason to suggest that this is because the native birds, mammals and predatory insects control the leaf-eating insects.*[1]

The task of revegetation on these farms is a slow, labour-intensive one. The New England area is a land of extremes. High-altitude and hundreds of kilometres from the coast, it is freezing in winter, subject to soaring temperatures and hot winds in summer, drought-prone, rabbit-infested and big. Unlike the small, hedgerowed farm holdings of traditional England, the properties of rural Australia are often thousands of hectares in size. The response to New England dieback and other signs of advanced land degradation in the Australian countryside, such as soil salinity and severe gully erosion, has necessarily been at a community level. The job of tree replacement is just too big for individual farmers and too urgent to be left to the government.

The consequences of hedgerow destruction and the various forms of tree dieback certainly highlighted the importance of birds and other fauna in 'pest' control. In short, the importance of biodiversity. Following hard on the heels of the still-being-digested news that pesticides bio-accumulate in the environment and that insects soon become resistant to them anyway, semi-natural habitat loss was another stark illustration of the benefits and importance of ecological balance, even in commercial environments.

Organic gardeners took note, and ideas of encouraging predators by providing habitat, food and water began to develop. Massive rural tree planting programs were also instigated.

In Australia, the Landcare movement was born. Its focus was the repair of degraded rural land, especially riparian zones (water courses) by revegetation organised at a community level involving the volunteer labour of landowners and other community members. As effective solutions were sought for these large-scale rural problems, the spotlight was increasingly on the importance of revegetation using endemic (those native to the particular region) species. Landcare groups began backyard nurseries where trees were propagated from locally collected seed of locally indigenous species. This understanding added a whole new dimension to the use of native plants, which had previously focused on using species that were simply native to Australia. From the fertile seed of Landcare grew Bushcare, Coastcare and Dunecare, all working with the same highly effective model of ecosystem repair by the local community.

I have focused here on particular situations in England and Australia, probably because I was aware of them at the time and because the hedgerow destruction in particular is a textbook case illustrating the catastrophic impact of semi-natural habitat loss. This lesson is of particular relevance to the idea of environmental gardening, as gardens can come into the category of semi-natural habitat if we design and plant them with this purpose in mind.

THE CHIPKO MOVEMENT OF INDIA

Simultaneously there were important experiences and crises all over the world, feeding like streams into the great river of environmental consciousness that was forming, and of which the organic movement was a part. A brief look at the Chipko movement that arose in India during the 1970s and 1980s will show the dynamic, effective and sophisticated response that came from this less modernised nation when their local forests, and therefore their ecologies, were being steadily destroyed by commercial interests.

Although the forests of India are a source of food, fuel and fodder to the rural people, the Chipko movement had an ecological basis. While earlier conflicts over forest use had occurred when villagers were denied access to the forest as a resource, Chipko was a response to the environmental damage resulting from forest clearing. The people living in the steep hill and mountain country of the Himalayas could read the signs of ecological crisis. Previously self-sufficient villages had to import food. They saw that this was related to loss of soil fertility in the forests. They also saw water sources go dry as the forests receded. Floods and landslides, so often referred to as 'natural disasters', began to happen in river systems that had always been stable. In a land as densely populated and economically vulnerable as India, such disasters are truly tragedies, in which many lives and much fragile infrastructure are lost.

Based on the Ghandian methods of non-violent resistance and the ideals of justice and ecological stability, the movement spread from its base in the Himalayas to states in the north, west, east, south and centre of India. The leaders of the movement were mainly women. They emerged all over India, performing hundreds of autonomous, local actions—an inspirational, democratic grassroots movement in the true sense of the concept.

The word 'chipko' means 'embrace'. They literally embraced the trees, putting their bodies between the tree and the raised axe. Their slogan was, 'What do the forests bear? Soil, water and pure air.' Their cause was recognised in the highest corridors of power in 1980, when the then Prime Minister Indira Ghandi ordered a 15-year ban on clearing the Himalayan forests of Uttar Pradesh, the state where the movement began. The movement continued to gather momentum, halting clear-felling in other areas and bringing pressure to bear on government to develop a natural-resources policy that recognised the needs of both people and the environment. In 1987 the movement was awarded the Right Livelihood Award (www.rightlivelihood.org/recip/chipko.htm), 'for its dedication to the conservation, restoration and ecologically-sound use of India's natural resources'.

In the Chipko movement farmers and gardeners acted to protect the ecology that has kept their lands fertile and productive for thousands of years of intensive cultivation. Their recognition of the interdependence of wild and domestic ecosystems for stability is perfectly expressed by the words of one of their leaders, Sunderlal Bahaguna: 'The solution of present-day problems lie in the re-establishment of a harmonious relationship between man and nature.'

In Australia, native vegetation continues to be cleared for farming, housing and forestry. From 1980 to 2000, 10 million hectares of native vegetation were cleared. It has been estimated that this clearing caused the loss (i.e. death) of 150 million birds alone. As this clearing has proceeded, the farmers of Australia have witnessed the same signs of ecological disintegration as the Indian villagers who embraced the trees to save them.

In the excellent booklet, *Birds on Farms: Ecological Management for Agricultural Sustainability*, Geoff Barrett writes:

In the temperate woodlands of Australia, where agriculture is a dominant land use, most of the complex natural ecosystems have been replaced by human-managed systems ... On many farms more than 90% of the native vegetation has been cleared ... The result has been a simplification of the ecosystem and a reduction in biodiversity ... the effect of this change can be seen clearly in the loss of many of the ecosystem processes that farmers rely upon. Soil protection has diminished as salinity and acidification have spread. Water production and purification are compromised. Greater severity and frequency of floods, droughts, and infestation by pests are other effects.[2]

CHAPTER 9

Dream team: birds, frogs and organic gardeners

DURING THE LAST QUARTER OF THE 20TH CENTURY THE ecological alarm bells were certainly ringing. The political backdrop for much of this time was that of the Cold War, with the nuclear arms race making total annihilation of man and environment seem a real possibility. There was a lot to grapple with in big-picture survival terms, and for most people, the immensity of such problems left them feeling powerless and vulnerable. One of the beauties of gardening is that it is so accessible. While the US and the USSR compared their nuclear warhead counts, organic gardeners absorbed the information about habitat loss, and moved from focusing largely on food growing without using artificial chemicals to introducing biodiversity concepts, although that is not what they were called at the time. From my observations, it began with the birds.

BIRDSCAPING

'Birdscaping' the garden became a theme of gardening books and articles during the 1980s. That is, planting to attract birds. Up until this time, the main relationship gardening literature had with birds had been how to *repel* them. But by the 1980s Rachel Carson's 'silent spring' had become a widespread reality. In 1962 she had written:

Over increasingly large areas of the United States, spring now comes unheralded by the return of the birds, and the early mornings are strangely silent where once they were filled with the beauty of birdsong. This sudden silencing of the song of the birds, this obliteration of the colour and beauty and interest they lend to our world have come about swiftly, insidiously, and unnoticed by those whose communities are as yet unaffected.[1]

In the UK, the loss of semi-natural habitat plus other changes to agricultural practices caused the populations of farmland birds to plummet from the mid-1970s to the mid-1980s. The birds of the English countryside had always been a vibrant layer of rural life, bringing song and movement and colour. Taken for granted since time immemorial, their decline in that single decade is an indicator of declining biodiversity to scientists, and an indicator of human stupidity to observers of human nature.

As the face of farmlands change, the importance of gardens as refuges for birds increases. Some species can spend their whole lives in our gardens, while many others come and go with the seasons.

Armed with the background information that gardens occupy more land than nature reserves in England, and that the sterility of modern agricultural practice is now entrenched, this placid statement about the role gardens can play as a haven for destitute birds takes on a new dimension, as gardens transform into lifeboats for birds and other small wildlife.

The recognition that our destruction of nature was making our farms and gardens into lonely places put the onus on us to re-make nature, in our backyards if that was where our power and influence lay. By implication, this meant increasing the use of native species, as the birds and wildlife of any region are adapted to the plants indigenous to that region.

The tradition of ornamental gardening and horticulture has tended to thrive on the excitement of discovering and nurturing the new and different, the exotic, the unusual, the spectacular. A combination of plant hunting in new lands and plant breeding for 'improvement' has fed this culture of desire for the last 200–300 years. Now, the time had come to make our gardens more than playgrounds for the gratification of our own tastes, inclinations and fashions. The glamorous flowers and foreign specimen trees, we discovered, were barren ground to most native birds, butterflies and their like. Gardeners and landholders turned to the native flora of their country or region, be it England, Australia or America, and discovered a wealth of simple, undemanding beauty. This beauty was multi-tiered: with it came the animation of bright parrots, tiny finches, soft butterflies, opalescent beetles, dew-jewelled spider webs—life.

As things tend to do, the idea of planting to attract birds became increasingly refined as experience was gained. Gardeners learnt that it is not enough to simply plant nectar-rich native species. Greater care and understanding is needed in plant selection if a *range* of birds is to be encouraged. For example, in Australia the popular large-flowered grevilleas attract large birds, whose dominance can keep away small birds. Small birds are not only delightful to watch in the garden, they also play a key role as predators of tiny insect pests, such as scale and aphids. Awareness that it was important to use plants that were locally endemic, not simply native to Australia, began to develop. In the UK, the Flora for Fauna website actually recommends endemic plants on the basis of your postcode. Inspired by this initiative, the Nursery Industry Association of Australia has developed a *Flora for Fauna* plant labelling and promotional package for its member nurseries, including an excellent website[2] to help gardeners select fauna-friendly plants suitable to their region.

Also, different birds have different nesting needs. While some thrive in a dense shrubbery, others need the hollows only found in old trees. In Australia, millions of old trees have been cleared since white settlement in 1788. Old-growth forests continue to be logged in spite of all the knowledge we now have. Grand, gnarled old trees on farms succumb to dieback, salinity and soil compaction, are then used for firewood. The trees we plant now, in our enthusiasm for repair, will not have hollows for 100 years or more. The hollows are formed by wood fungi and termites, both of which are frowned upon by the average landscape manager. Hollow old trees are certainly not common or popular or quick to grow in the suburbs. The gardening solution has been to devise custom-made nesting boxes. Organisations such as the Gould League have developed expertise in this complex field, but it is not altogether unproblematic, and maintenance is needed. As is always the case, what nature did so effortlessly takes enormous amounts of collective human energy and ingenuity to replicate. And even then it is, more often than not, inferior.

As well as species selection, the planting structure of birdscaped gardens was found to be important—vegetation layers are essential in designing a garden to suit a diversity of birds. Trees, shrubs, small wildflowers, clumping plants such as native grasses are all needed in a garden that aims to feed and house a diversity of local birds. A water supply, be it birdbath or pond, was another element and environmentally-minded gardeners have found themselves installing these since the mid-1980s. And the beloved pet hunter, the cat, became a matter for the conscience.

These developments did not happen overnight. What I am hoping to show here is a little of the process behind the evolution of organics in the last 40 years. Sadly, it has generally been motivated by bad news, of which there was much more in store during the 1990s. And in truth it was not so much the birds who made us install ponds. It was the frogs.

THE KERMIT FACTOR

'Frogscaping your garden' doesn't roll off the tongue quite so nicely as 'birdscaping'. However, few organic gardening books would now dare go into print without including a section on how easy (and important) it is to install a frog pond. Our memories are short, and you are forgiven for forgetting that this was not always so. What happened? When and why did the frog and its need for a backyard pond enter our consciousness?

Sesame Street's endearing muppet, Kermit the Frog, has been immortalised by his long-suffering observation, 'It's not easy being green.' His words were truer than he, or his makers, knew.

The alarming news of an international decline in frog numbers came to light in 1989. Herpetologists at the First World Congress of Herpetology realised that many of their colleagues from faraway countries shared similar anecdotal evidence that frog numbers were down. This disturbing sign of yet another weak link in the integrity of the global ecology was particularly pertinent as frogs are regarded as being like the canary in the coalmine in terms of environmental damage. While the sensitivity of the canary was used to detect gas leaks in coalmines before the miners were affected, frogs are known to be acutely sensitive to the subtlest of changes in their environment. Being amphibians, their environment is both terrestrial and aquatic. The sinister twist in the Kermit Factor was that frog numbers were down in areas of pristine habitat, such as the wet tropical rainforests of north-eastern Australia. The problem, it seemed, was not just one of habitat loss or pesticide contamination, although where these occurred, they certainly affected frog populations. The impact of our lifestyle was proving insidious. A definitive cause for the tragic decline of the world's frogs has yet to be isolated, though many theories are being tested.

In the meantime, the frog crisis contributed to a growing awareness of both the importance of and the decline in overall biodiversity on this spinning Earth which is our home. Frog ponds, which incidentally had been championed by Permaculture for the previous decade, became mainstream as the increasingly influential gardening media (always on the lookout for a new angle) embraced the idea. Perhaps predictably, the mania for frogs in the backyard had its downside for frogs in the wild, as tadpole collecting began to deplete remnant urban frog habitats of their population base. Frog-pond books and articles now caution against tadpole introduction—let the frogs find the pond, is their advice.

Ponds, of course, also bring myriad insects, lizards, birds and other creatures that need a drink or a watery home, or like to eat the things that ponds attract. Water is a life-magnet, essential to biodiversity. The organic garden was more and more seeking to replicate the wildness that gardens had originally been a refuge from. The haven from the wild was becoming a haven *for* the wild. The garden was coming full circle. But these ideas were still fringe. It wasn't until the 1990s that the trickle down into the mainstream took hold. As we shall see, more bad news was needed before the mindset of the mainstream could make this shift.

DURING THE 1980S ANOTHER ISSUE FOCUSED THE SPOTLIGHT on an aspect of biodiversity we have not yet looked at. The biodiversity issue wasn't (and isn't) confined to 'wild' ecologies. Threats to the diversity of the very food that sustains us emerged as debate raged around the introduction of plant patenting legislation (also referred to as Plant Breeder's Rights or

CHAPTER 10

Fears for our food

PBR) in Australia during the early 1980s, and the tightening up of older laws in this area worldwide. The agribusiness juggernaut was consolidating. I was a horticulture student at the time, and was acutely aware of the major impacts these issues were having on the culture of organic gardening in Australia. The seed-saving movement was born, stimulated by a sense of urgency to preserve non-hybrid and 'heirloom' varieties of vegetables and grains in particular.

THE POLITICS OF SEEDS

Plant Breeder's Rights, it was feared, would mean that those with the money to invest in the lengthy and expensive process of plant breeding and patenting would gain domination as they gradually came to control the seed supplies of global food crops. The laws made it illegal to propagate from patented plants for commercial purposes unless a royalty was paid to the originator of the strain. The increasing involvement of multinational corporations in the seed trade was changing the face of agriculture. Small seed companies were increasingly bought up by corporations who were also involved in plant breeding. It was feared that many of the traditional seed lines would be lost as the dictates of multinational economics became the determinant by which varieties were made available, rather than the varietal needs of particular regions and communities that smaller companies had served.

One aspect of this was the increasing dominance of hybrid seed lines. Agricultural dependence on hybrids bypassed the 'problem' of farmers saving their own seed in the first place, as hybrids are either sterile or produce seed of low viability and vigour which is not true to type. The controversy over the successes and failures of the Green Revolution[1] in the Third World played into the debate, demonstrating the pitfalls both of losing food-crop biodiversity and of taking the power to grow his own seed crop from the ordinary farmer.

Another spectre that loomed up out of the emerging agribusiness ogre was the news that the same multinationals seeking to dominate the seed trade were the producers of gardening and agricultural chemicals. The 'vertical integration' of the business of food production was under way. Vertical integration means that a business expands in such a way that it is no longer based around a single product line, but seeks to own a whole set or suite of products that relate to and support each other. For example, a seed company would not just trade in seeds. It would also trade in the fertilisers and pesticides needed to grow that seed crop.

It does not take a great leap of logic to see that it would then be in the best interests of that company to market these products together. And you do not have to be a conspiracy theorist to wonder if they might even tailor their products to depend on one another. For example, a high yielding rice or wheat hybrid will certainly raise productivity, but to make sure the yield is maximised, such-and-such fertiliser is recommended. And having invested good money in your seed and fertiliser, regular applications of this pesticide will insure your investment against insect attack. Such companies, it was feared, would make all effort to ensure the dependence of the consumer on their product, creating a monopoly in which the consumer, once 'locked in', had little room to move. The consumer in this case is the farmer, as the home gardener is small fry in the seed trade. Incidentally, being small fry means not being very well looked after. Steve Solomon, founder of Territorial Seed Co. in Oregon (a regionally-based, gardener-oriented company), has the perspective of an insider. 'Lacking experience,' he writes, 'the home gardener can be sold their leftovers, older poorly germinating seedlots, "suspect" lots (ones that produce numerous off-types) — stuff that one frank upper-executive once described to me as "the sweepings off the seedroom floor".'[2]

Traditionally, most farmers saved their own crop seed from season to season. All over the world, in obscure valleys and on remote mountainsides, these farmers lived independently, creators and guardians of humanity's diverse and nutritious agricultural food supply. The economics of seed was highly localised. The varieties they grew were adapted to local conditions and met local needs. In the new, globalised system, large-scale economic efficiencies would take precedence. An audit of the global food-crop gene pool is not included in the annual reports of multinational corporations, just as the number of crop pests eaten by dragonflies, frogs, lizards and tiny birds is not listed. And as we know, that which is not valued is lost.

As usual, those with the passion and courage to defy Goliath took the matter into their own hands. Small, family-run companies specialising in open-pollinated seed started to appear, and seed-saver groups and networks developed, encouraging gardeners to save the seeds of the vegetable varieties best suited to their own area, and share them via community-based networks. In this way the big seed companies and government bureaucracies were bypassed, and at the same time, attention was focused on gene-pool preservation and evolution.

In the US the issue is older than in Australia. Kent Whealy founded the Seed Savers' Exchange in 1975, with the grand total of 29 members. Today, membership is more like 8000. The Exchange is headquartered at Heritage Farm, an 890-acre property in Iowa. Here, some 24 000 rare vegetable varieties are grown in carefully managed gardens. The significance of the seedbank is internationally recognised and works collaboratively with the Vavilov Institute in Russia (once the home of the world's greatest seedbank). In the orchard 700 of the 8000 named apple tree varieties that existed in the US in 1900 are grown. These are all that can be tracked down. The remaining 7200, it seems, are extinct. A herd of about 80 rare, white cattle is also kept, helping preserve a wild breed that roamed the British Isles before the birth of Christ. Globally, the herd numbers only 800.

In Australia, Jude and Michel Fanton established the Seed Savers' Network in 1986. They describe it as 'a community-based organisation supported wholly by subscription and the work and goodwill of many friends and volunteers'. By 1999, the Network had received 4500 varieties. These are maintained in a seedbank, in on-site trial gardens and in the gardens of members all over Australia.[3]

Being an organic gardener was becoming more complex and more holistic. It no longer meant simply using pyrethrum instead of DDT and spreading compost instead of NPK fertiliser. Caring and concerned gardeners continued to take responsibility into their own hands—or into their own backyards, as it were—hoping to look after their own health, their family's health, and the health of the planet. This meant acting on new information in whatever ways were possible—such as installing a frog pond, planting flora with fauna in mind, and saving their own vegetable seeds.

Stranger and stranger

All these concerns existed before the genetic engineering debate arrived with tidal wave-like impact. Along with global warming, during the 1990s, the GMO (genetically-modified organism) debate brought many major environmental issues to the attention of people who had not previously taken much notice of conservation issues or organics. Biotechnology quickly became a flashpoint for protest against globalisation and what was perceived as its attendant undermining of community and environmental values, including the freedom to choose in the most basic arena, that of the food we eat.

The mega-companies who now dominated the global seed and agrochemical markets were at the forefront of biotechnology. Brian Tokar, in his book *Redesigning Life?*, writes:

> *Farmers face an unprecedented concentration of ownership in the seed and agrochemical industries, a problem that has very closely paralleled the development of genetically modified crop varieties ... The late 1990s saw a heretofore unimaginable wave of corporate mergers and acquisitions in virtually every*

*economic sector, and now the three pivotal areas of seeds,
pharmaceuticals and agricultural chemicals are increasingly
dominated by a small handful of transnational giants, all
centrally committed to the advancement of biotechnology ... By
1999, five companies — AstraZeneca, DuPont, Monsanto,
Novartis and Aventis — controlled 60% of the global pesticide
market, 23% of the commercial seed market and nearly all the
world's genetically modified seeds.*[4]

Opposition to genetically modified foodstuffs exploded in the lucrative marketplace of Europe when it rejected US foods containing GMOs, ultimately causing a major rethink in this US-based industry. In India, farmers and the public reacted in 1998 to Monsanto's secretive establishment of field trials of GMO cotton by crop burnings. In the same year, Monsanto acquired 26 percent of Mahyco, India's largest seed company. The community response was an intensification of the revival of seed-saving which had been spreading through village India since the early 1990s. Here in Australia, the island-state of Tasmania led the anti-GMO movement, with the government declaring a moratorium on trials of genetically engineered food crops, as it sought to maintain the 'clean, green' image that gave it excellent entree into the fussy European market, which incidentally, was increasingly demanding certified organic food.

In amongst these issues which were either blatantly affecting biodiversity through habitat destruction, or threatening food-crop diversity and even safety via business trends and biotechnology, a couple of other very bad news environmental stories made the headlines in the

1980s and 1990s, shocking the world and putting politicians on notice to deliver solutions.

BETWEEN US AND THE REST OF THE UNIVERSE
Most of us had never heard of the ozone layer until they told us in the mid-1980s that it had a hole in it, and had generally become ragged. CSIRO online describes the situation succinctly:

> *Ozone depletion in the upper atmosphere is the result of human-produced chemicals, such as chlorofluorocarbons (CFCs) and halons. Depletion is especially severe over Antarctica in spring, causing the highly publicised 'ozone hole'. However, at all latitudes away from the equator, the layer of ozone that protects us from the harmful radiation of the sun is thinner than it was in the late 1970s.*[5]

The Montreal Protocol, signed in 1987 by 180 countries, was an international agreement to phase out 96 ozone-depleting chemicals. It came into force in 1990, however the guilty gases last a long time, so even with complete phase out, the ozone layer is not expected to return to normal until 2050. The full implications of the increase in exposure to radiation being experienced by life on Earth are not known.

Not so long after we had thrown out all the aerosols in the cupboard, we were informed that there were other changes taking place in the atmosphere. Of all the things to mess up, the atmosphere was perhaps the worst. It is all that separated, and protected us, from the rest of the universe. We had definitely taken it for granted, and wanted to keep doing so. But the Greenhouse Effect, like ozone depletion, could not be ignored. It seemed that while we had been distracted by fears of the nuclear winter that was modelled during the latter years of the Cold War, global warming had been quietly happening all around us. The 1990s was the warmest decade on record, and 1998 the hottest year. 2002 became the second hottest. Although the Kyoto Protocol on climate change was signed by 84 countries in 1997, the solutions are proving much harder to achieve than those relating to ozone depletion.

The list of eco-tragedies of our making has become a very long one. There are many I have left out, including the peculiar phenomenon of Mad Cow Disease (BSE), which along with the GMO debate contributed enormously to the demand for organic food in Europe and the UK. By the year 2000, faced with repeated evidence of the interconnections that thread so intricately not just between all life forms but throughout all that *supports* life on Earth, almost 40 years after *Silent Spring*, organics was well and truly mainstream. It had also matured into a holistic system with recognition of its role in wider issues of environmental protection and repair.

PART 4

In the environmental garden

CHAPTER 11

Starting point: know what you have

WITHIN ANY GARDEN THERE ARE KEY COMPONENTS THAT the gardener works with. Soil, climate (including water), design and plant selection broadly cover most bases. As I have already said, this book is not a gardening manual, nor is it a design manual. There are many, many of those available based on a wide range of approaches to gardening. These days there is generally at least a tokenistic nod towards the environment, in the form of using organic techniques. My hope is that as you absorb the ideas in *Beyond Organics*, you will be able to adapt all that technical information out there and use it as needed to help you garden with nature's point of view uppermost in your mind. Ultimately that is the point of view which will meet your needs in any case.

In order to use mainstream gardening information in this way, you need to know the underlying practicalities of what goes on in the environmental garden. Inspiration and understanding have little use unless they lead to action, action that expresses care and responsibility. As you go about your gardening, your environmental point of view will affect the decisions you make. It is important to be clear about what you hope to accomplish. The points below are like guidelines, or thought lines that run through the activities inherent in environmental gardening:

• Understand what was there before development and base your garden on these raw materials (i.e. soil, climate, plants).

• Grow plants that suit your area. Minimise the use of high-need plants (including lawn), and keep them grouped together.

• Remember that ecologically, the boundary fence is a mirage. This boundary is constantly being crossed in both directions by water, wind, nutrients, soil, leaves, seeds, pollen, insects, birds, reptiles and so on. Each time you think about introducing or applying something to the garden, ask yourself, *Where did it come from, where will it go and what will it do?*

• Know that every element of your property is habitat, from the cracks in the path to the crown of the tallest tree. Maximise the habitat and feeding opportunities for small, native wildlife that are compatible with people.

• Encourage biodiversity through planting, design and management methods, with a focus on local species.

• Avoid all plants with the potential to become feral, and avoid gardening practices that encourage weed growth *outside* your garden (e.g. nutrient and water run-off).

UNDERSTAND WHAT CAME BEFORE

No garden is a blank slate. Whether the land was cleared last week or 5000 years ago, its ecological history is far older than the oldest of gardens. The piece of land you call your own was once home to a dynamic, self-sufficient natural ecosystem.

In well-established cities, where the suburbs stretch beyond the horizon, enclosing a patchwork of luminous lawns, rows of roses, 'suitable' trees and easy-going shrubs, not to mention all the roads and built bits, it is hard to imagine what came before. Villages and settlements creep out to become towns, towns swell into cities and in human time, the changes are all so gradual and cross-generational that the memory of what was passes into history.

In all but the most extreme of environments around the globe, there was once the soft scratching of birds in the undergrowth, the struggle of seeds to survive, the gentle slither of snakes and lizards, the busyness of insect societies, perhaps the antics of arboreal mammals in trees, the thudding of great, soft-footed kangaroos in the warm, dry bush or the stampeding of bison across the vastness of prairie grass. And no-one needed to look after any of it. No watering systems, no fertiliser or spray regimes, no designers, nurserymen or hardware men advising which product to buy.

There were flowers, with birds dipping their perfectly shaped beaks into the nectar, tiny bees buzzing for pollen and honey, moths at night, and perhaps fruit bats following the flowering season, from north to south in Australia. There were trees, maybe stunted and gnarled or tall and full of grace, entire ecosystems in themselves, providing homes and food, their roots diving deep and spreading far in the layers of soil.

These days we call whole, intact ecosystems 'wilderness'. Once upon a time, that's all there was. Even in your backyard.

There are two reasons why your garden's original ecology matters. One has relevance to your gardening; the other has relevance to life on Earth. In relation to your gardening, if you work within the framework of the original ecology, your job as gardener will be a whole lot easier. From the point of view of the living planet, there will be many more opportunities for environmental balance, and life.

Soil

I have grown up in Australia, a land where the soils are old and thin and 'exhausted', and the climate prone to extremes that make gardening difficult. Well, this is how we interpret the situation. Australian soils, for example, are renowned for having low phosphate levels. Needless to say, this depleted soil has been a source of frustration. As mentioned in *Chapter 6 — High-need gardens*, however, a vast array of plant species evolved and grew on these soils without the addition of composts or fertilisers. In fact, all Australian native plants fall into this category — and the census for the Sydney basin alone outnumbers those plants originating in England. Is a soil phosphorous-deficient to a plant that doesn't need much phosphorous? Is a soil nutrient-poor to a plant that has evolved clever ways of extracting nutrients with the help of soil bacteria and fungi? Is the climate too dry for a plant whose under-standing of dryness has been perfected in the structure of its every cell? Are torrential downpours and high humidity problematic to plants possessed of sturdy flowers and drip tips on the ends of their leaves for easily shedding water? No, these 'difficulties' are of our own making, as we strive and struggle to grow plants that don't belong.

In spite of living in a country that boasts one of the world's most diverse and interesting native flora, superbly adapted to where we live, most Australian garden owners set themselves the uphill battle of growing plants that don't thrive easily on our soils or in our conditions.

The obsession with roses is notable. Their unsuitability to many parts of Australia keeps nurseries in business, as failed rose growers are repeat buyers. Sydney, the most populous city, has a lush, humid climate beloved of fungi and insects, largely sandy soils that are low in nutrient and unable to hold moisture, and a mild, virtually frost-free winter.

Maintaining a healthy rose in such conditions requires high-input gardening—feeding, watering, pest and disease control and, often, plant replacement. In return, these demanding plants give little back to the environment. Their flowers are mostly human creations in terms of colour and form, offering scant sustenance for pollen and nectar feeders; other feeders, such as caterpillars and aphids, are pests, and must be gotten rid of, whether organically or chemically, thereby removing a link in the food chain of insect feeders. The structure of the bushes is likewise shaped for human purposes of neatness, cut-flower production and 'hygiene'. For example, they are kept open to allow ventilation as a discouragement to fungi; however, this pruning doesn't create nice dense habitats for nesting and hiding amongst the thorns. A rose bush in these conditions is little more than a battleground to which the gardener is devoted for the occasional reward of a lush flower.

This is but one example of an ill-suited plant that is continually used in gardens because of the glamour, hype and romance in which it has become embedded. It is not a beautiful plant; it is an ugly plant that throws up a few lovely flowers as it struggles for health in the wrong environment. Yet people put up with these frustrating and unattractive shrubs year after year in a climate and on soils that are home to one of the world's most diverse flora. By finding out about the soil and climate you have, and the plants that grew in those conditions without the help of any human hand, you give yourself the starting point for gardening in a way that gives back to and supports the environment rather than taking from it. By developing an understanding of the raw materials of your landscape and trying to work as much as possible within the parameters set by those materials, you begin to allow a harmony to re-evolve.

WHAT ARE THE QUALITIES OF YOUR SOIL?

Almost every gardening book starts by saying that soil is the foundation of it all, and emphasises the importance of good soil preparation. This preparation usually means modifying the soil to suit the plants you want to grow. Gardening manuals are full of advice on how to 'improve' soil, how to change it. The ideas of improvement and change are generally based around fulfilling your fantasies and dreams of creating a picture-book garden. Then comes page after page of the obligatory information on composting, fertilising, worm farming, mulching, digging, not digging, clay-breaking, transforming sand (which they comfortingly say is good for carrots), raising pH (pretty easy), lowering pH (harder), keeping up the organic matter, drainage solutions and so it goes on.

Inspired by the pretty pictures and practical line drawings, plus the enthusiasm of the author for all this hard work, you make a shopping list and walk out into the offending backyard. It is a yard that is now guilty of many soil offences that need correcting before the pleasures of garden beauty can be enjoyed. How did it ever manage without you? Well, it was all quite simple really. It had no unrealistic ambitions, it lived within its means and it played host to a team of life forms whose interactions maintained its health under normal circumstances, and patiently restored its health following abnormal circumstances (such as flood, drought, landslide, fire).

This gardening book has no information on soil improvement, but it has information on soil and the ecosystem of the soil world. I have decided to pedantically resist the term 'improvement' unless it refers to soil that has really been damaged, and needs repair. Otherwise, when meeting the demands of high-need plants such as vegetables and roses, I prefer to think of it in terms of the plant's special needs rather than the soil's innate inadequacy. This will be looked at later in the book.

In the meantime, every garden comes with soil, and that soil will have certain properties which are acceptable to some plants and unacceptable to others. Find out about the soil's properties, and then find out which plants accept these properties. There are bound to be many to choose from. *In an environmental garden, these should form the basis of the garden's planting design.* Plants with needs that are not met by your soil should be kept to a minimum. They can be grown in pots, and in a selected area that is gardened more intensively such as a vegie patch.

The qualities of soil that influence its interaction with plants include its texture, structure and pH. The texture and structure influence nutrient and moisture holding and release capacity, while the pH (scale of acidity – alkalinity) affects nutrient availability.

SOIL TEXTURE

An understanding of soil texture is important. The soil's texture is a result of the parent rock from which it is derived, so it is an innate characteristic that is hard to change. Many lone battles are fought by gardeners attempting to change soil texture in order to meet the needs of certain plants they want to grow. These plants are always going to be hard work, as the effort to transform a soil's texture is never complete. Better to grow plants that are adapted to the texture you have, than work hard to change geology.

Soil textures lie between the extremes of beach sand and pottery clay. Think of it as the genetic makeup of the soil. To give yourself an idea of what sort of soil you have, try rolling a moistened handful into a sausage. The strength and stability of the sausage indicate the texture; that is, the more sand there is, the less stable the sausage, the more clay, the more stable. A balance between the two makes for easier gardening. If you have a soil at either extreme, this will have a greater impact on your plant selection, and it is advisable to do a little research before wasting money and time on plants that will die.

SOIL STRUCTURE

Soil structure is changeable and is influenced by the gardener's activities, the impact of weather, and anything that interacts with it. If the texture is equivalent to genetic makeup, then structure is equivalent to your body's health, and in the same way, is influenced by its experience of the world. Structure is often referred to as 'friability'. It involves the way the soil is held together, or not held together, in little bundles called aggregates.

Hold out both your hands. Into the right hand imagine some soil collected from just below the leaf litter of a rainforest. Let's say its texture is a sandy-loam. It is high in organic matter and living organisms or their influences, is moist, dark and has that healthy, wholesome earthy smell we associate with well-made compost and rotting logs beneath the forest canopy. It has known only the soft padding and hopping of marsupial feet, the slow dripping of rain filtered by layers of leaves and bark. The protection of constant leaf fall has kept it in the dark and cool, at a relatively stable temperature. This soil lies in your hand in little clusters of particles, which cling together, held by the delicate forces of soil chemistry. This is soil of 'good' structure. It holds nutrients and it releases them readily to plant roots. It holds moisture and releases it readily to plant roots. It has within its form an ideal proportion of air-filled and water-filled spaces. It feeds and supports the dense, fecund growth of rainforest that rises up from it so strongly. It is part of a system that works well together as a team.

In your left hand imagine soil from the same location after the forest has been converted to cattle pasture for a few years. Remember, the texture is fixed — it is still a sandy-loam. The soil collapses in your palm, looking as you might feel after a stressful year in the office with a tyrant boss and impossible deadlines. The particles do not hold together in nice teams anymore. They fall alone, or else sit tense and fixed in hard, concrete-like lumps, much as your back might feel after the stressful year in the office, during which the benefits of good team work have been dissipated by bad management. First came the men with hard boots and chainsaws to bring down the great trees whose whispering canopies shielded the floor from baking sun and pounding rain. Bulldozers and trucks followed, crushing air and moisture out of the soft, good soil, and scraping off the protective layers of leaf and twig. Stripped bare and naked, the full force of the sun sucked out its water and baked it hard as in a kiln. This alternated with drenching rain, no longer filtered by leaves and bark, but falling hard on the back of the sun-baked soil, which rejected most of it, so that run-off carried silt away, muddying the rivers and streams that connect a network of gullies. Wind also tore at the naked body of the earth, carrying away a fine dust from its surface. Tractors came with implements to rip through the good soil, so that pasture grasses could be sown for the new life of this place. Fertilisers were spread also, and their acidity killed most remaining earthworms and other delicate lives that had been part of the soil's good-health team. Shallow grass roots then matted the upper layer of the soil, but no deep foraging roots opened up the subsoil for water drainage and aeration, so a hard pan formed under the tight layer of grass roots. When the torrential rains came, they could not penetrate this hard pan, and the topsoil flooded, squeezing out the air once more and suffocating plant roots and tiny creatures, all of which breathe. The cattle came also, with their great weight being grown for the butchers, and their hard hooves, so that each step was a burden on the tired back of the soil. Treated thus by the world around it, the soil's structure gave way. All this stress took its health, broke its back as it were, and the structure collapsed, unable now to support either itself or the team of plant and animal life which once lived and interacted within and around it without need of any fertilising, cultivating or watering.

When considering soil structure and therefore soil health, the soil should be thought of as a living, breathing organism, not as inert grains of dirt. The rules for maintenance of soil structure are simple, and can be gleaned from the scenario given above. Organic gardening books also have sound information on soil maintenance. Don't forget, in an environmental garden, soil structure will need the most attention in the vegetable patch, as the turnover of plants and therefore the demands on the soil are constant. To summarise:

- Protect soil from compaction and weather extremes. Minimise impact by machinery, human activity and animals, and insulate from the sun, rain and frost with a deep layer of organic mulch.

- Avoid waterlogging by not overwatering and ensuring drainage is adequate.
- Minimise disturbance and cultivation. In cultivated parts of the garden, such as the vegie patch, use standard organic gardening practices including high organic matter levels; no-dig techniques or minimum tilling (e.g. only when soil moisture is medium); crop rotation; and use of organic mulches.
- If irrigation is necessary, use a system that delivers the water gently (i.e. fine spray, drip or seepage).

SOIL PH

Most people know that pH refers to a soil's level of acidity or alkalinity. They are unlikely to know that pH refers to the negative log of the soil's hydrogen ion activity. Without this understanding they probably don't realise that the pH scale is logarithmic, meaning that each unit of the scale indicates a tenfold change. Therefore, while 6.0 is 10 times more acidic than 7.0, a reading of 5.0 is 100 times more acidic than 7.0. So, the more extreme the reading, the more extreme the change.

Another thing that most people don't understand about pH is the effect it has on nutrient availability. They usually don't realise that the reason some plants are 'acid lovers' is not actually because they are lovers of acid but because they are lovers of iron. In an acid soil, you see, iron becomes more available to plants. Most plants will grow quite well in a pH range on either side of 7.0, which is neutral. Those that are fussy are the ones that like high-ish amounts of a nutrient that becomes less available towards either the acid or alkaline extremes, as in the example of the acid lovers. To continue with that example, the availability of iron decreases as pH rises above 6.0, so that acid lovers such as azaleas and camellias are likely to show deficiency symptoms even in a neutral soil. Below 6.0, however, most other nutrients decline in availability, as they also tend to do at the other end of the scale as alkalinity rises beyond neutral 7.0.

So, although pH can be adjusted by addition of chemicals or modified toward neutral by organic matter and worm castings, this need for modification is not a one-off, it will continue. It is important to know your starting point, and work with this in your plant selection.

Let me illustrate by example. As I have mentioned, I grew up by the beach in Sydney. I have childhood memories of the azalea and camellia plants my mother popped in, hoping for their vibrant colours in the soft green shade that the trees and ferns of the garden made. Without exception they sickened and died. At the age of 16 I became passionate about gardening and acquired a pH testing kit, which, believe it or not, was an exciting moment. I squatted on the gritty sandstone, placing little scoops of light, grey soil on the testing plate, blending it with the indicator, dusting the mixture with white powder, watching and waiting for the colour change. The powder darkened, and kept darkening to a dull purple. The reading was, as I remember it, higher than 8.0. Most books simply say that sandy and coastal soils tend to be acid, whereas they can carry the limey residue of crushed sea shells, pushing the pH up, not down, way beyond neutral. Until then I had been following the general-purpose instructions that characterise gardening manuals. Consequently, I had added lime to the soil when I planted irises! They did not thrive, in spite of my attentions. If I had known more, I may have realised that Mum's doomed attempts at growing azaleas meant there was no need to add lime, as the chlorosis (yellowing) of their leaves is an indicator of alkalinity.

While in most parts of the garden you can simply choose plants that like the existing pH, you may need to manage the pH in your vegetable patch. The presence of earthworms neutralises pH as their castings are neutral, so pH adjustment should involve encouraging a healthy worm population. For more details on pH in the vegie patch, refer to your organic gardening reference book, and *measure the pH first*.

Damaged soils

Be aware that even some endemic plants show deficiencies on soils which have originally supported a lush plant and animal ecology. There is a good chance that such soils may need rejuvenating due to loss of structure, leaching from high rainfall and/or watering practices, plus loss of the natural nutrient cycling system. On building sites topsoil is often removed, compacted and replaced with cheap fill or left with a legacy of building waste such as lime, sand or blue metal. Salinity can be a problem in both rural and urban soils. Waterlogging from leaking drains or swimming pools also affects soil structure and life. Some soils have a history of high inputs of synthesised fertiliser and/or pesticides, making them hostile to both plant and animal life. The restoration of organic matter to such soils is vital and standard organic soil improvement practices can be adopted. Organic matter and soil life have a remarkable capacity to restore health and dynamism to soils, but this takes time and encouragement. These soils need you to provide optimum conditions of moisture, organic matter and aeration, plus protection from new stress. Mulching is vital.

Ultimately, if your garden's green life is based on the plants that originally occurred there, the need to fertilise will be minimal. Gardening books and the gardening media will always tell you to fertilise, even your native plants. Remember that they have to fill their pages and their airtime with advice, or else they are out of a job. They are also likely to be selling advertising to fertiliser companies, and telling you how to garden without these products can also put them out of a job.

An appropriate slow-release fertiliser at planting time is a good idea, as your soil is unlikely to be in a virgin state and this is the most vulnerable time for your new plants. Mulching is important for helping establish a garden ecosystem in which natural nutrient cycling develops. Aim for your plants to become as independent of fertilising and soil adjustments as possible, but give them the help they need to reach that point.

KNOW YOUR OWN SOIL

Gardening books do not know your soil. Gardening books these days are designed for an ever-greater market, and as a result their bland generalising is less helpful than ever. The majority of them are the creations of international publishing houses that are creatures of the globalised book trade. They do not know where you live.

An understanding of the roles and nature of soil texture, structure and pH will set you on the right track to managing your garden in an environmentally sound way. Choose plants that will be happy in your soil type, not plants that crave what your soil does not have.

CLIMATE

We each know the climate we live in, its patterns and vagaries, as these affect us in many parts of life beyond our involvement with the garden.

Again, in order to minimise the needs of your garden, choose plants that are suited to your climate. Microclimates exist within gardens, and can also be consciously created by the gardener. The simplest examples are windbreaks, deep shade and lightly coloured, reflective walls. Irrigation is really an attempt at climate modification, though it is not usually thought of in that way. Whenever you water you are generating artificial rainfall to support plants that need more than the natural climate supplies. A hothouse is a more elaborate and obvious form of climate modification.

The more you attempt to modify the climate in order to grow plants from other areas, the more input is required and the opportunities for negative impact on the environment increase. Salinity in irrigation areas and the suburbs and the high incidence of pests and diseases in a hothouse are examples of problems arising from climate modification in gardening and agriculture. Pest and disease problems in hothouses have led to extreme use of chemical controls, including soil gassing between crops to kill all life, and resistance of insects to sprays, resulting in the ineffectiveness of some highly toxic and residual poisons. Illogically, more spray tends to be applied, which only speeds up the development of pest resistance.

These problems are not only ecologically expensive, but also economically expensive, both in their implementation and if they result in a need for further repair. One 'solution' to the problem of soil pathogen build-up in commercial hothouses has been to take the soil right out of the system and use hydroponics. Fed on nutrient solutions in a controlled environment, there is a soullessness about these perfect-looking flowers and vegetables. It is as though the lack of contact with the vibrancy of a living, breathing ecology starves them of a dimension that cannot be pinned down.

The creation of microclimates has its place in a garden. However, the motto 'all things in moderation' needs to be applied. I will tell you the strange story of a bizarre example of enthusiasm gone wrong in relation to microclimate creation. At one stage I was a Permaculture enthusiast. During this time I visited a Permaculture property on a cold plateau of fog and frost and wind and occasional snowfalls that rises gloriously behind the subtropical NSW mid-north coast. The property owner had worked hard to create maximum self-sufficiency using Permaculture principles. He showed us around his lake aka heat bank/light reflector/aquaculture, his vegie patch cum chook tractor system (incidentally, it was one of the best I have seen), his coppiced firewood-producing trees (also doing the job well) and so on. Then he loaded us into a 4WD truck and we set off into the forested hills. Finally we pulled up and walked along a small track. We reached a clearing where we were proudly presented with a sad-looking clump of banana trees. Nearby was an above-ground swimming pool full of rain water with a system of pipes whose purpose I don't fully recall beyond irrigating the banana grove. This was a frost-free microclimate, our host announced, and yes, he had harvested some bananas. His drive for the ideal of self-sufficiency and clever Permaculture ideas had created this odd, inefficient, ambitious project. No more than an hour's drive down the road was Coffs Harbour, where an abundance of banana plantations tumble down the steep slopes in the subtropical climate. In those days roadside stalls sold the fruit for as little as 20 cents a kilo.

The message about climate is the same as for soil, and it is simple.

Grow plants that like your climate and aim to minimise the need for modification, including watering. If the rainfall is low or there are seasonal drought times, the plants that originally grew on your land developed mechanisms to survive this aridity. Perhaps they have fleshy, succulent, water-storing leaves, stems, roots or bulbs. Perhaps the leaves have layers of protective, hard-walled cells that help the plant retain moisture, or stomates that close in the heat of the day, to minimise transpiration, or leaves that align themselves to hang at right angles to the sun to reduce exposure like the eucalypts. Or maybe they have hardly any leaves at all, like cacti that have done away with the luxury of leaf area for photosynthesis. Others, like the Australian red cedar *Toona australis*, lose their leaves during the dry season; or have grey leaves that reflect the light; or go completely dormant in the hot dry summer, like the fairy-flowered cyclamen of Turkey.

Whether the climate is hot and dry, humid and wet, cold and windy, or whatever, the endemic plants will have adapted minutely to the climatic conditions of your area. If you choose from these plants, the need to modify the climate through watering, frost protection, wind protection, shade provision, etc will be virtually nil. Most places experience weather extremes, or 'events' at some time. These may come in the form of lengthy drought, flooding, late frost or high-speed winds. At these times, your ecosystem garden will be stressed, as would a natural ecosystem, and any help you can give to the garden when conditions are abnormal should be given. But in general, as with food needs, these plants will be largely independent of you in terms of coping with climate conditions.

WATER

Rain falls from the sky for free, becoming our water supply. It is a gift that we take for granted, as seems to be our way with things that exist without needing either effort or dollars from us.

More than 40 years ago, Rachel Carson in *Silent Spring* made this stark accusation about the carelessness with which we treat the water that sustains all life: 'Of all our natural resources water has become the most precious … In an age when man has forgotten his origins and is blind even to his most essential needs for survival, water along with other resources has become the victim of his indifference.'[1]

Perhaps we are finally heeding Carson's caution. There is much talk and angst about water use and quality these days. In drought-prone Australia, the droughts have become worse. In 1995 Sydney's drinking water became undrinkable due to bacterial contamination. Summer or dry-season water restrictions and user-pays meters have become almost standard. Awareness of both our dependence and our indifference has been forced upon us. For many people, it is this single issue that is leading to a gardening rethink, and from my anecdotal observations, low-water gardening is commonly equated with being environmentally responsible. As we have seen in previous chapters, water availability is only part of the story for farmers and gardeners, as complex issues such as salinity and algal bloom are also caused by land management and water-use practices.

Solutions to the basic issue of water shortage in the suburbs are being refined and developed as the need becomes more acute. These include grey water (and black water) re-use and on-site collection of rainwater in tanks, both important parts of environmental living and gardening. Your garden's water needs depend on which plants you choose to grow. If you are inclined towards food production, the garden's water needs will be up. If that is so, installation of a tank or re-use system to meet the needs of food growing should be seriously looked at to minimise the garden's negative environmental impact.

However, there is more to water collection and storage than meets the eye. Although we are beset by water shortages, 74 percent of the Earth's surface is covered in water, and there is a whole lot more below the surface, in the soil, a whole lot more in the air, and yet more still held within all living organisms. The problem as we perceive it, of course, is that most of the 74 percent is unusable, as 70 percent of it is salty ocean and a few more percent is frozen as ice cap and glacier. Nevertheless, the perspective shifts when we think in terms of the cycling of water, which restores all these sources back into usefulness within the great patience of time.

Returning now to the microcosm of the garden, most of the water in it is invisible. Unless it has died, your garden is full of stored water, as is a natural grassland which may appear dry, as is a multi-layered forest, where no water collection, storage or distribution are apparent. Water is all through the soil, and because it is all through the soil, it is also all through the plants. It is also in the air. Plants tell you very quickly and clearly when the soil and air are short of water relative to their needs. They start to collapse. If the water is not replenished, they eventually reach the point of no return, known in the trade as 'permanent wilting point' (PWP). And yet, how often, even in the severest of droughts, do the plants of natural systems reach PWP?

I used to work as a guide in a subtropical rainforest national park, taking groups of day trippers along its cool tracks. I was astonished one day when a woman asked a very obvious question. The year was, I think,

1995 or 1996 and eastern Australia was deep in the grip of the worst drought on record. After walking for some time under the canopy of giant trees, soft with moss and hung about with a lushness of vines and ferns, she quietly asked me if anyone watered the forest. An image arose in my mind of park workers lugging hoses up and down the hill, and draining their bath water in the direction of the forest. Somehow keeping a straight face, I told her there was no need to water the forest, as it is a self-sustaining system, and she asked no more.

Inherent qualities of water collection and storage are part of your garden. Herein lies a fundamental part of the environmental gardener's water rethink.

One of the pioneers of organics, Sir Albert Howard, expressed his appreciation and learning from nature about soil water with great humility and respect in *An Agricultural Testament*. Howard was an English agricultural scientist who spent many years working in India. It was there that he formulated a deep understanding of how the processes of nature interact with the processes of agriculture. On the flow of water through the soil he wrote:

The rainfall in particular is carefully conserved. A large portion is retained in the surface soil: the excess is gently transferred to the subsoil and in due course to the streams and rivers. The fine spray created by the foliage is transformed by the protective ground litter into thin films of water which move slowly downwards, first into the humus layer and then into the soil and subsoil. These latter have been made porous in two ways: by the creation of a well-marked crumb structure and by a network of drainage and aeration channels made by earthworms and other burrowing animals. The pore space of the forest soil is at its maximum so that there is a large internal soil surface over which the thin films of water can creep. There is also ample humus for the direct absorption of moisture. The excess drains away slowly by way of the subsoil. There is remarkably little run-off, even from the primeval rain forest. When this occurs it is practically clear water. Hardly any soil is removed. Nothing in the nature of soil erosion occurs. The streams and rivers in forest areas are always perennial because of the vast quantity of water in slow transit between the rainstorms and the sea. There is therefore little or no drought in forest areas because so much of the rainfall is retained exactly where it is needed. There is no waste anywhere.[2]

But not all the water from rainstorms makes that slow subterranean seepage to the sea. Depending on the density and nature of vegetation on a piece of land, a proportion is intercepted, captured, collected, by plant roots. We know how they seek it out, blocking pipes and drains, following dampness between rocks and paving stones, diving deep into the lightless water table or growing shallow if our irrigation methods are shallow. Succulent root systems store water as an insurance against seasonal dryness or even worse, fire. Bulbs, tubers, rhizomes, the lignotubers of the mallee, all hold water in the cool, dark, soil, where sun and flame cannot reach. Above ground, the stems, trunks, leaves, flowers and fruits of the plants are all users, holders and transporters of water. Their structure is minutely adapted to the water patterns of their place of origin. From the structure and arrangement of each cell, to their overall size, shape and texture, each plant part tells the story of water availability in the place it evolved.

As a horticulture student I recall pressing my eye to the microscope as I gazed at a section of an oleander leaf. I had known oleanders were hardy, but now I knew why. That leaf section was made for survival. It was made tough. The outer layer, the cuticle, was extra thick. And there wasn't just one cell layer protecting the moist insides of the leaf. As I recall, there were two or three. The little holes through which water transpires (stomata) were sheltered in 'crypts', bay-like formations lined with hairs and protected from the sun and wind of the unkind world. This means that when moisture escapes via the stomata, it is trapped in the hairy crypt, and most likely will ultimately be reabsorbed rather than lost to the drying atmosphere. I also knew that all oleander parts were deadly poisonous. This was truly a shrub with a fortress mentality. Having harboured a grudge against oleanders since they had been a feature of my high school grounds, I came away with a new respect. Oleanders had obviously been through a lot as they evolved against the odds in distant Africa.

Everyone is familiar with the water-storing adaptations of cacti and succulents, which is why we think of them when we think water-wise gardening. But there are thousands of non-desert plants that can be grown without needing supplementary watering. The plants and the soil know better than we do how to manage and conserve water. It is our task to make use of this knowledge in our approach to gardening.

This rethink means that environmental gardening virtually makes *water a non-issue. Water doesn't need to be a gardening problem.* The water issue is largely taken care of by plant selection and grouping. Using the principle of minimum climate modification, and remembering that water is part of climate, approach plant selection according to these priorities:

1. The majority of ornamental plants in an environmental garden should be indigenous—once established, their needs are largely met by natural rainfall.

2. Non-indigenous or exotic plants should be ones whose water needs can largely be met by natural rainfall.

3. Keep high-need plants to a minimum. This includes lawn. Group them together and use cultural methods that minimise water wastage e.g. maintain good soil structure, use mulch, irrigate efficiently.

As well as plant selection, these water-wise strategies should be used:

• Mulch, mulch, mulch—a depth of 75 mm is ideal; any deeper than this and the mulch itself will absorb large amounts of water.

• Plant trees, shrubs and other perennials at the time of year when rainfall and/or lower temperatures mean less watering is needed for establishment. Ensure that during establishment the plants have deep and regular water, if not from the rain, then from irrigation. Once established, they should manage without watering except in times of extreme dry.

• Water at a cool time of day, or at night.

• Irrigate efficiently—install fixed micro-spray or drip irrigation with a timer in preference to using a moveable sprinkler that is easily left on too long, and probably waters areas that don't need it e.g. the driveway. Porous soaker hoses made from recycled tyres are an excellent system that can be placed under the mulch to deliver water straight to the root zone.

Additionally, on-site water management can be taken a step further by installing a rainwater tank and water-recycling system.

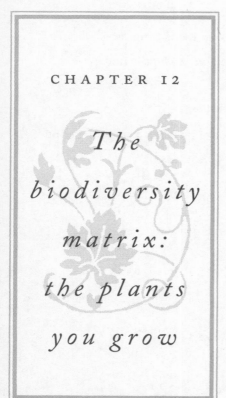

CHAPTER 12

The biodiversity matrix: the plants you grow

PLANTS ARE THE LINK, THE CONNECTORS. THEY bring together the inanimate energies of the elements and transform them into life. From the sun, the air, the water and the earth, plants draw the building blocks of life, combine them, and grow. And through their growth processes, they enable all life to flourish. They are first base on the food chain, as nothing else can eat light and pull nutrients in solution from the soils. Their vast root systems stabilise and shape the ground we walk upon, also keeping fresh water systems pure. Their constant pumping of ground water is an integral part of the water cycle all life depends upon, and it is their breath that makes the air breathable, as they inhale carbon dioxide and exhale oxygen. This short but significant list gives only the fundamentals of all that plants contribute to our survival and quality of life, as they bridge the vastly different worlds of earth and sky.

Plants are the focus of the environmental garden. It will chiefly be your choice of plants that determines the nature of the garden's interaction with the wider ecology. There are two reasons for this — what the plants need, and what the plants give. If the plants are high need, that is, dependent on regular supplementary feeding, watering and protection, they are on the take, and will reduce the garden's overall positive environmental contribution, even if you use organics. The more the plants give, in terms of food, shelter, habitat, nutrient cycling, soil stabilising and so on, the more they maximise the garden's environmental positives. They are a resource for the environment, rather than a sink. If these same plants are low need, that is, virtually independent of you, the ecological profits go up even more. Ecology is basically the economics of nature. The words ecology and economics even have the same Greek root, which is *oikos*, meaning household.

The plants most likely to push up the environmental profits are the ones that grew naturally in the garden's region before there was any development. In places where agriculture and gardening are very old, this might include plants that have been integrated into the ecology over many hundreds or thousands of years.

The idea of growing local species has been steadily gaining popularity since the mid-1980s, pushed along by concerns of declining biodiversity and, in Australia at least, the revelation that even native plants can become environmental weeds. In terms of biodiversity protection, there are two angles that plant selection influences. The first is the plants themselves; the second is the fauna who use those plants.

PLANTS FIRST

As we know, when people set up their habitat (houses, farms, roads, shopping centres, sportsgrounds, hospitals, parliaments, schools, industry...) entire ecosystems are often destroyed. Parks and gardens are planted out with all sorts of plants from all over the world, many of which have probably been tampered with by plant breeders to maximise their decorative appeal to one pushy animal species—*Homo sapiens*. The plant species that originally grew on that land become marginalised. Remnants often hang on in obscure places, such as graveyards and rural roadsides, as well as reserves.

Or for obscure reasons. For example, Sydney has the army and infectious diseases to thank for much of the Sydney Harbour National Park. Battlements intended to protect this vast land from invasion look out towards the dramatic harbour entrance from amongst pink-barked angophoras and coastal heath. On North Head is the Quarantine Station, where boats landed carrying emigrants feverish with typhoid, cholera and smallpox. They were then taken aside after their long, cramped journey and held isolated a little longer, above sapphire bays where fairy penguins waddled and flocks of parrots squabbled in the gum blossom. If not for these institutions 'locking up' the bushland, the areas would no doubt have become exclusive waterfront suburbs providing homes for the wealthy, rather than homes for our flora and fauna.

However, obscure places and reasons aside, the plant diversity of areas where people live is vulnerable. Plants with a narrow distribution range become extinct or endangered because people are conditioned to an aesthetic that rejects them. In Australia, the perceptions of the settlers were grounded in the European landscape. The Australian vegetation looked dull, rough and ragged. Occasionally, new eyes saw it differently.

Husband and wife team, Walter Burley Griffin and Marion Mahoney, the prize-winning designers of Canberra from the United States, were brilliant architectural and landscape designers. They saw the inherent and enigmatic beauty of the Australian flora and were appalled at its wanton destruction. On the foreshores of Sydney Harbour the Burley Griffins developed a subdivision that retained the natural vegetation and blended the houses with it architecturally. The gardens were the bush, which they recognised as already perfect.

Edna Walling was another designer with a deep respect and appreciation for the wisdom of nature in achieving a landscape design aesthetic. She wrote: 'Again, the amateur gardener who considers his planting effects from the ecological point of view, that is, the study of natural association of plants, will make better landscape pictures than those who take no thought for the matter.'[1]

Indigenous plants are ideally suited to life on the soils and climate of their origin, and as such harmonise with each other and the world around them. This is where they belong. They know how to interact with the watertable, the winds, the droughts, floods, rocks, soils, micro-organisms and fauna. If the soils are relatively low in nutrition, these plants have either found ways of managing on those nutrient levels or of extracting otherwise unavailable food through physiological adaptations, such as proteoid roots and/or associations with other forms of life, such as mychorrizal fungi. For example, proteoid roots are found on plants in the family Proteaceae. On the roots of these plants there are dense masses of very fine, white root hairs. The enormous surface area of these feeder roots increases the plant's ability to extract nutrients from the soil. Mychorrizal fungi are soil fungi that live in association with plant roots, accessing otherwise unavailable soil nutrients for the plant, especially phosphorous and potassium.

Their adaptation to the climate means indigenous plants have had to survive even the greatest extremes over thousands or millions of years, or else die out. In a nutshell, by growing local species you minimise the need for inputs and interventions such as fertilising, watering and protecting.

The relationship of plants with so-called pests is a little more complicated. An abundance of insects feed on Australian plants. Eucalypts could be seen as a sort of vertical buffet for a vast and varied collection of hungry arthropods. The leaves are often spotted with gum tree scale and lerps. Dramatic-looking, stinging-haired cup moth caterpillars chew around the leaf edges, while cleverly camouflaged case moth larvae simply poke their heads out of their twiggy cocoons to feed. The peculiar stick insects are also content when nibbling up high in a gum tree. In fact, so often do gum leaves have ragged edges that there is even a looper caterpillar whose camouflage is to look like the ragged edge of a gum leaf. Many more creatures feed under the bark and in the wood, as well as the root system. Fungi are also a part of the ecology of plants and their root zone, and are an important food source for a wide range of fauna.

Obviously, the plants and the feeders have evolved together, so it cannot be said that using local species reduces insect attack. However, they have all survived together, and part of that balance has been the abundance of predatory fauna which keep the plant feeders from overwhelming the plant. With the 'pests' come their predators—birds, lizards, frogs, spiders and other insects. Even though there are plenty of 'pests', there is seldom a need to control them as long as you are not aiming for perfection in every leaf and bud. The story of New England dieback in *Chapter 8—Habitat holocaust* is worth recalling in this context. The balance was lost, and native pests and the secondary diseases that followed them did play a major role in the death of many, many trees.

By planting local species you help keep the local ecology alive. In his book, *Australian Planting Design*, Paul Thompson puts reasons for growing native plants succinctly:

The preservation of species by raising awareness and increasing our knowledge about Australian plants is as compelling a reason for growing them as I know. The chance of a new discovery and the possibility of broadening the interests of others are bonuses. Conservation of plants leads to support for all the other creatures that rely on those plants.[2]

This 'support for all the other creatures that rely on those plants' is another way that local species promote regional biodiversity.

PLANTS FOR ANIMALS

When we talk about attracting wildlife to the garden, we are mainly talking about birds and invertebrates. Next on the list would come reptiles, frogs, and finally, small mammals. Birds are used as an indicator species for biodiversity of both plants and animals, and it is birds that are the most common subjects of research in this field. So by gardening in a way that attracts birds, we will automatically lift the plant diversity and are likely to raise the overall faunal biodiversity of our garden. It is, therefore, to research on birds that we turn to learn what sort of planting scheme is best for biodiversity.

The Birds on Farms Survey was undertaken by Birds Australia between 1995 and 2000. The survey aimed to 'assess whether the environmental work carried out by organisations such as Landcare was drawing birds back into rural landscapes.'[3] It also sought to identify the key factors that increase bird diversity, and formulated 10 guidelines for attracting birds to farms. Interestingly, this approach to land management for biodiversity has its starting point in finding ways of making agriculture sustainable, rather than nature conservation.

The first guideline recommends that for agricultural sustainability 'local native vegetation should cover at least 30 percent of the total farm area'. The second guideline is 're-create local conditions'. Both these guidelines clearly state that local vegetation is essential for care of the land, which by implication means optimising conditions for biodiversity. Remembering that birds are an indicator of overall biodiversity, the findings show how important the presence of local plant species is. For example, the survey revealed that more tree cover means a significant increase in native bird diversity and a dramatic decrease in exotic birds. For every 10 percent more trees there were 7 percent more native birds and 21 percent fewer exotics. This effect was even greater when the trees were local species. On farms where more than 80 percent of trees were local natives, the diversity of native woodland birds was 43 percent greater. Natural regeneration as opposed to tree planting also favoured these birds. Diversity of woodland birds was 21 percent higher on farms where the regeneration had been natural. By contrast, where exotic trees had been planted, the small-foliage gleaning native birds that feed so effectively on many insect 'pests' were 26 percent less diverse, while exotic bird diversity increased five-fold.

Thinking back to the stories of specific plant – animal relationships in *Chapter 4 — The meaning of flowers*, these figures make very good sense. The more common birds and insects tend not to have such specific requirements, and are the ones that thrive in human environments. These are few, however, compared with the total number of species originally living in an area. Exotic plantings can also be directly detrimental to biodiversity. For example, shrubs with winter berries such as hawthorn and pyracantha encourage currawongs, which are nest predators. In a healthy woodland ecosystem only about a third of nests succeed in rearing young, so further reductions have a serious impact on small-bird populations. The diversity of naturally regenerating vegetation can also be compromised by exotics. In northern NSW, the camphor laurel *Cinnamomum camphora*, a magnificent tree from China, has invaded farms, stream banks and forest margins. It produces an abundance of small, black berries, which birds feast on, spreading the seeds as they move around. The birds feed on these plentiful and accessible berries in preference to the fruits of the native laurel species in the remnant rainforests of this once jungle-clad landscape. In this way, the regeneration of the native laurels has been reduced, while the camphor laurel invasion is out of control.

The specific requirements of particular birds and insects do not need to be known to the average gardener in great detail. You won't be introducing them to the garden, they will be finding it. Follow two ground rules and you have a good chance of success in optimising both the vegetative and faunal biodiversity within your garden:

1. use local species; and
2. use a mixture of them.

Like creates like. Complexity creates diversity. Local plants support local animals.

This need for complexity brings us also to questions of planting *design*, which is a vital aspect of plant selection.

VEGETATION LAYERS

To maximise your garden's benefits to the environment, its planting structure needs to be multi-layered, just as anywhere aiming for high-density living makes use of multistorey accommodation. The layers are broadly classed as trees and understorey. Trees create a canopy layer, often at two levels, while the understorey is multi-layered, being made of tall, medium and small shrubs, climbers, grasses, groundcovers and herbs. Ferns and epiphytes are also part of the understorey in wet forest ecosystems. As well as the more obvious aspects of providing for different food, protection and nesting requirements, the structure of the plant layer affects temperature, humidity and light intensity, all of which are particularly important for insect populations.

The structure of layers in the natural environment is dictated by soil and climate conditions. On exposed, coastal sites with shallow, leached soils the low-growing shrubs dominate, with no tree canopy at all. Grasslands are often graced by groupings of trees where the water table is higher. In Australia, forested lands tend to include a diverse understorey of grasses, shrubs, creepers, ferns and epiphytes, plus, of course, the overstorey of tree canopy. By sourcing local species for the garden, you will end up with a structure that reflects the original.

TREES

Visually, trees provide architectural structure to a garden. Edna Walling takes delight in pointing out that the common perception of trees as being space hungry is wrong:

> *How dull a treeless garden can be ... I shall never forget one*

client: 'I want you to get me half a dozen choice shrubs,' he said pompously.

'Whatever for?' I said ...

'To plant in my garden, of course,' he said snappily.

'What, without some trees to go with them?'

'Trees grow too big,' he said.

'They don't take up as much room as shrubs,' said I, and once again I had to explain this little thing. And before I'd finished he had decided, being a man of action, to have all trees and no shrubs!

'What, no shrubs?' I said, and then I had to explain that I needed some shrubs to make a picture. His energy was fading.

'Oh, do as you like,' he said, throwing up his hands.[4]

The space trees use, once established, is largely vertical space. They are the high-rise component of the garden habitat. In Australia, eucalypts are the most important tree genus in the wild, and ditto in the environmental garden. In the ecological profit-and-loss sheet, they give and give and give, and their needs are easily met due to the sophistication of their adaptations to survival. Their blossoms, nectar, pollen, leaves, seeds, sap and even their wood are all food sources to myriad birds, insects and mammals. The food matrix on a eucalypt is complex, as the feeders themselves attract many predators. For example, the sap-sucking psyllid and its sweet covering, the lerp, provide important meals for many small birds, predatory insects and even arboreal mammals. Lerp and psyllid lovers include pardalotes, bellbirds, welcome swallows, tree martins, ladybirds, assassin bugs, lacewings, wasps and sugar gliders.

Birds also feast on the wood- and bark-feeding grubs that are invariably part of the eucalypt ecosystem. Nesting sites, nesting materials, perches and shelter are all provided in abundance by eucalypts, especially old trees with hollows.

In spite of Edna Walling's assertion that trees are space-savers, there are a multitude of reasons why people don't plant trees in their gardens, especially large ones, which most eucalypts are. There are, however, small eucalypts which can be used in virtually any garden. Some of these are the multi-stemmed mallees of arid Australia, with their stocky form and often large, brilliantly coloured blossom and equally large and uniquely shaped gum nuts. Also, dwarf selections of some eucalypts are now coming onto the market. 'Little Snowman', a small-growing variety of *Eucalyptus pauciflora*, the snow gum, is an example. It is the result of the passion and dedication of native-plant enthusiasts Bill Molyneux and Sue Forrester of Austraflora, an innovative company that has done much to develop Australian plants for maximum garden performance. Such trees may not be native to your area, but the role of eucalypts is so important that if the local eucalypts are unsuitable for your garden due to size, opt for a small-grower from elsewhere.

After eucalypts, choose local tree species that are practical for your garden. In your planting layout, move away from the 'specimen tree' mentality. The specimen tree is an isolated tree whose main purpose is to create a visual aesthetic that appeals to humans. Nature prefers trees in groupings. By planting trees close together, even placing more than one in the same hole, their size will be inhibited, which can be an advantage in small gardens. The tree grouping can have more than one species, bringing variation into the structure as well as the food supply of the planting.

The table on pages 182 and 183 is a list of 'gum' trees suitable for small gardens. Strictly speaking they are not all gums, and these days, neither are they all eucalypts. The term 'gum tree' is used generically to refer to the hundreds of species that are botanically classified as *Eucalypts*, *Corymbias* and *Angophoras*. To those in the know, a gum tree has loose peeling bark, as opposed to other species which have rough, furrowed or stringy barks. An ironbark, for example, is not a gum. To complicate matters further, those in charge of botanical naming have reclassified the trees that were once either *Eucalypt* or *Angophora*, introducing a third genus, *Corymbia*. So, what was once *Eucalyptus ficifolia*, the red flowering gum, is now *Corymbia ficifolia*.

SMALL GUM TREES FOR SMALL GARDENS

(FROM THE GENERA ANGOPHORA, CORYMBIA & EUCALYPTUS)

NAME AND DISTRIBUTION	HEIGHT (M)
Angophora	
A. bakeri (Narrow-leafed Apple) NSW	10
A. hispida (Dwarf Apple) NSW	5
Corymbia	
C. ficifolia (Red Flowering Gum) WA	10
C. ficifolia Summertime™	6
C. ptychocarpa NT, WA	10
C. 'Summer Beauty'	8
C. 'Summer Red'	8
Eucalyptus	
E. baeuerlenii NSW	8
E. caesia (Gungurru) WA	6-9
E. cinerea (Argyle Apple) NSW, Vic	10-15
E. conferruminata WA	6-9
E. crenulata (Victorian Silver Gum) Vic	10
E. curtisii (Plunkett Mallee) Qld	7
E. erythrocorys (Illyarrie) WA	8
E. forrestiana (Fuchsia Gum) WA	6
E. gillii (Curly Mallee) SA, NSW	6
E. gregsoniana NSW	5
E. kruseana WA	5
E. leucoxylon 'Rosea' NSW, Vic, SA	15
E. leucoxylon 'Magnet' Euky Dwarf™	6
E. macrocarpa (Mottlecah) WA	3
E. mannifera 'Patches' Little Spotty™	5-7
E. melanophloia (Silver-leaved ironbark) Qld, NSW	10
E. olivaceae 'Lorikeet' Summer Scentsation™	4-6
E. pachyphylla (Red-budded Mallee) SA,WA,NT,Qld	2-5
E. pauciflora 'Frosty' NSW, Vic, Tas	4-7
E. preissiana (Bell-fruited Mallee) WA	1.5-3
E. sclerophylla (Scribbly Gum); NSW	9
E. scoparia (Wallangarra White Gum) Qld, NSW	8-10
E. stellulata 'Aemon' Little Star™	3-7
E. stricta (Blue Mountains Mallee) NSW	7
E. youngiana (Large-fruited Mallee) WA, SA	8

This chart is adapted from a table on the website of the Society for Growing Australian Plants.
The original was compiled by Brian Walters.

Blossom colour and notes

White; flowers profusely
White; flowers profusely, may be grown as a large shrub

Blossom may be pink, red, orange, white; very spectacular; grafted specimens are dwarfed
  and best for obtaining specific colours eg Summertime ™
Red
White, pink or red; best for tropical areas
Pink; hybrid between C. ficifolia and C. ptychocarpa; only available grafted
Red; hybrid between C. ficifolia and C. ptychocarpa; only available grafted

White; rare in nature; cold hardy
Pink, red; 'Silver Princess' is a weeping cultivar with larger flowers and fruits
White; attractive blue/green, rounded juvenile leaves retained
Green; some success in eastern areas
White; attractive foliage
Green; flowers profusely
Bright yellow; some success in eastern areas
Yellow; red fruits a feature
White; retains rounded, juvenile foliage on the mature tree
White; rare in nature; cold hardy
Greenish-yellow; attractive foliage and bark; best for temperate and semi-arid areas
Pink, red; very attractive. NB the ordinary species grows taller
Deep pink, red
Red; some success in eastern areas
Masses of creamy blossom. NB this is a dwarf cultivar – the ordinary species grows much taller
White; attractive silvery/grey foliage
Bright yellow in large clusters; perfumed
Cream to yellow; best for arid and semi-arid areas
Masses of creamy blossom, colourful peeling bark. Also sold as Edna Walling® Little Snowman ™
Yellow; adaptable; reasonably successful in eastern states
White; beautiful trunk with scribbly markings
White; beautiful weeping foliage and white trunk
Masses of creamy blossom
White
Red, yellow, cream; large blossoms; suited to semi-arid areas

OLD TREES, HOLLOWS AND HABITAT

Magnificent birds such as cockatoos, rosellas, rainbow lorikeets, some owls and kookaburras, as well as small birds including some pardalotes, tree creepers and shrike-thrushes, nest in the hollows of old trees. Hollow trees are rare in the suburbs. It means having mature trees, generally with some dead branches or damage in the trunk that may make the tree 'unsound'. Apart from the fact that you cannot plant such a tree, the risk of having dead tree limbs in the backyard is something most people prefer to avoid. So if you want these creatures to be at home in your garden, you will have to make the homes. This also applies if you live in an area where it is possible to encourage arboreal mammals such as gliders, bats and possums (not all possums are brushtails). Tree hollows or their equivalent are a necessity.

Providing homes for these animals means installing nest boxes that copy the natural hollows they prefer. It is essential to source local information for this, as it is a specialised area. The Gould League publication, *The Nest Box Book*[5], gives construction and installation information for Australian birds and arboreal mammals.

Management and after-care of the boxes is vital, so this direction should only be taken if the time, skills and motivation are there. If you wish to attract these animals, you'll also need to make sure their food and water needs are met, so research is the best idea. More on nest boxes a little later.

There is one more arboreal mammal that Australians may want to encourage. That is the koala. As a child in Sydney, I remember stories of koalas in people's gardens on the Northern Beaches peninsula around Pittwater. This group is all but gone, due to dogs and other pressures of urban living. However, I believe there are still some koalas in the bush around the suburb of Avalon. As all Australians know, koalas are fussy eaters. They eat gum leaves, yes, but only a limited selection of species. The following list gives some of the eucalypt species preferred by koalas.

E. camaldulensis River red gum

E. citriodora Lemon-scented gum

E. grandis Flooded gum

E. maculata Spotted gum

E. melliodora Yellow box

E. microcorys Tallowwood

E. nicholii Small-leafed peppermint

E. parramattensis Drooping red gum

E. populnea Poplar box

E. propinqua Small-fruited grey gum

E. punctata Grey gum

E. robusta Swamp mahogany

E. saligna Blue gum

E. tereticornis Forest red gum

E. viminalis Manna gum

THE UNDERSTOREY

If the tree canopy is likened to the high-rise buildings of a city, the understorey resembles the CBD. The understorey is the hub, a zone of diversity and activity where the great mass of the population go about their various lives. While you might find three or four tree species in a hectare of natural woodland, there can be 30 or more species in the understorey, supporting an equally diverse array of fauna. However, in the world of plant politics, it is the trees and the impact of tree loss and decline that has attracted the most attention. Typically, the big guys have hogged the limelight, so that major revegetation efforts often focus on tree planting.

In the garden, however, understorey plantings tend to dominate. There are many opportunities to develop this most important zone in an environmental way. The roles the understorey plays are key contributors to environmental health. Guideline Number 9 of the Birds on Farms Survey highlights this fact: 'Maintain shrub cover over at least one-third of the area within a patch of farm trees.'[6] The survey showed that farms with understorey had 31 percent greater diversity of native woodland birds, including a 24 percent increase in the small woodland birds known as foliage-gleaners. On these farms noisy miners were 78 percent less likely to be present, while the diversity of ground-nesting native birds was up to three times greater. The noisy miner is an aggressive native honey eater which often becomes dominant at the expense of smaller birds.

UNDERSTOREY HOMES, FEASTS AND PRIVATE HABITS

Flowering shrubs are like food halls for garden wildlife. They make up the multi-layered understorey, providing nectar and pollen-rich flowers plus seeds, fruits, leaves, sap and gum in a safe, dense, sheltered environment. A mix of tall (3–6 metres), medium (1–3 metres) and small (less than 1 metre) shrubs caters to a wide range of creatures and their various needs. The majority of Australian plants are shrubs and it is within this group that the most colourful and dramatic flowering is found.

The insects that are attracted by the plants will in turn attract insect predators, such as birds, predatory invertebrates, lizards, frogs and at night, bats and possibly small arboreal mammals, creating a general buzz and flurry around the shrubbery. With some thoughtful plant selection, year-round flowering is possible. The inclusion of winter-flowering shrubs helps keep nectar-feeding birds in the garden while there are few insects to feed on. This means the birds are there, ready to revert to an insect-based diet when the warmer weather brings back the bugs and beetles.

A diverse understorey is vital for butterflies, of which Australia has around 650 species. The adults are nectar feeders and forage on flowers in bright, sunny places. Their larvae are fussier about their meals, however, and eggs are laid onto particular plants whose leaves or buds they like to eat. For some, such as the endangered Richmond Birdwing and piceatus butterflies, only one plant species will do.

The Richmond Birdwing, one of Australia's largest and most striking butterflies, only lays its eggs onto one type of rainforest vine. It lives in southern Queensland and northern NSW, an area which was clad in vast tracts of subtropical rainforest until clearing for agriculture reduced these rich ecologies to tiny remnants dotted here and there amongst the rolling hills of pasture grass and cropland. The colourful female has a wingspan of up to 15 cm, while the male is known for the splendour of his glamorous green, yellow and black attire. Each larvae needs to eat at least 1 square metre of the leaves of the Richmond Birdwing vine *Pararistolochia praevenosa*. The food problem is compounded by the growing of a similar vine, the Dutchman's pipe *Aristolochia elegans*, in gardens. This vine attracts the butterfly, but is toxic to the larvae. More than $1 million dollars of Federal Government funding plus a community-based campaign involving school children are part of the effort underway to save this once-common butterfly. One focus of the campaign is the role of gardens, with gardeners being encouraged to remove the exotic vine and plant the native one.

The piceatus blue butterfly is perhaps even more particular. Its larvae depend on one species of bull-oak, *Allocasuarina luehmannii*. Old-growth trees are required, as eggs are laid on twigs 4–7 metres above the ground. A particular species of ant also needs to be present, as it has a symbiotic relationship with the larvae. Ideally, the trees have some dead, horizontal, hollow branches, as the caterpillars feed on new growth at night, and hide in hollows by day.

It is clear that for these and other creatures the presence of indigenous plant species in a complex ecology is essential. While the piceatus larvae need old-growth trees, its butterflies must also feed. The floral richness of understorey plantings sustains them.

The lively honeyeaters, buzzing bees and coloured butterflies are all quite visible and/or noisy, so you will know they are there. But remember that there are many more subtle meals going on in the understorey, including nocturnal ones.

Native wasps are important predatory and parasitic insects in Australia. They are often very small and unlike the feral European wasps, go unnoticed. Some native wasps feed on the nectar and pollen of flowering shrubs, such as tea trees, and will not fly more than a few hundred metres from this food source. Certain species lay their eggs in grubs which feed on the roots of grasses. The eggs hatch and the wasps-to-be devour the soft body of the grub, thus helping control leaf eaters like the Christmas beetle. Christmas beetles have been a major factor in eucalypt dieback on farms. Once the role of creatures such as these wasps is understood, the importance of having regular understorey plantings becomes obvious. If the wasps will only fly a few hundred metres from their shrubs, the grubs beyond that zone will be out of reach, they will keep eating the grass roots, and many more beetles will hatch.

Under cover of darkness in the cold of winter, sugar gliders seek out gum on the branches and trunks of wattles when buds, flowers, fruits and insects are harder to come by. If you live near to some natural bush with the old trees that gliders nest in, they may find your wattle gum. Ringtail possums sometimes live in the suburbs, making their nests in the dense, tangled shrubbery or climbers rather than tree hollows. They avoid coming down to the ground, preferring the safety of continuous canopy for travel. I live in a suburb with some semi-wild parkland close by. I have seen a ringtail on the fence at night, and another one dead on the pavement below the power lines in the morning. My neighbour says they nest in the dense tangle of native vines that grow on her fence. Flying foxes, often called fruit bats, have more freedom of movement and if there is a colony within flying distance, they will find the flowering and fruiting shrubs and trees in your garden, pollinating as they gorge on the sweet offerings. If you plant with these gentle mammals in mind, the opportunity for them to survive and visit your garden exists.

WHAT TO PLANT

Diversity continues as the main theme. Showy, nectar-heavy shrubs such as the grevilleas, callistemons, melaleucas, leptospermums and banksias are all popular garden plants. There are many species and varieties to choose from and they bring a multitude of nectar-feeding fauna. However, some of the larger nectar-feeding birds can be aggressive and dominate the shrubbery at the expense of the smaller foliage gleaners, so it is important to provide a refuge for the smaller birds by interplanting with other shrubs that are less attractive to the honeyeaters. For this purpose, use plants that have pollen-rich flowers and nutritious seeds, such as wattles. Australia is home to more than 800 species of *Acacia*, so variety need not be a problem. They come in practically all shapes and sizes, from groundcovers to sizable trees, and occur all over Australia, from the desert to the rainforest. Shrubs with relatively insignificant flowers also fit in here. *Allocasuarinas*, *bursaria* and *dodonea* are examples. From an aesthetic point of view, this approach encourages the use of plants which have strong foliage and architectural value to complement the more obvious beauty of those with bright flowers.

The structure of the shrubbery is important and will depend on your particular climate and environment. Ideally it will be at least two shrubs deep, preferably three, and will include a blend of sizes. Think of it as a hedgerow: a dense, continuous planting with few gaps. Remember also that this is an understorey—that means there are also some trees. The architecture, textures and colours are the raw materials of the overall design, and the opportunities for creativity here are infinite.

The small shrubs, those that grow no more than 1 metre high, offer a wealth of flowering and fruiting across the seasons. Many of the heaths and alpines fall into this size group. They are ideal for borders, rockeries, as fillers, and planted in masses as features in their own right. These plants can be used to create graceful drifts and ribbons of colour and life. Here you find many of the *correas*, *croweas*, *darwinias*, *eriostemons*, *eremophilas*, *boronias*, *pimeleas* and *thryptomenes*, to name a very few.

Herbs, grasses and groundcovers make up the ground storey of the ecological CBD. Groundcovers are used extensively in landscaping for their visual effect and also as weed inhibitors and soil protectors. They form a living mulch, and as such help keep the soil conditioned and healthy. There are many prostrate forms of Australian plants available, often with excellent flowering qualities as well as forming dense mats of foliage. The grevilleas have proved a rich resource in the development of native groundcovers for gardens and landscaping. Other genera usually associated with the larger shrubs also have prostrate species — *acacia*, *banksia*, *leptospermum* and *melaleuca* all include groundcover species and cultivars.

A diverse and continuous understorey is essential in a garden which is based around inviting nature to thrive. The Australian Flora for Fauna website is an incredible resource for plant selection when planning the environmental garden. It is an initiative of the Nursery Industry Association of Australia. Have a look, at www.floraforfauna.com.au.

In summary, when choosing the understorey include plants that:
• Range in height from groundcovers to tall shrubs.
• Produce seeds, an important protein source for birds.
• Have flowers rich in nectar.
• Have flowers rich in pollen.
• Flower at various times of the year, providing a steady nectar supply across the seasons.
• Have dense, prickly foliage for protection from cats and other predators, especially at nesting time.

THE GREATNESS OF GRASSLAND

Native grasslands are one of Australia's and the world's most endangered ecosystems. It is in the grasslands that many of the small, annual wildflowers grow, creating intermittent splashes of colour and variety within the sea of waving grasses. Diminishing bird populations accompany their decline, as many small birds depend on the seeds of native herbs and grasses. Some of our most delightful and attractive birds, the finches and fairy wrens, are amongst these. Larger native birds dependent on grasslands include the common bronzewing pigeon and the peaceful dove.

A 1996 press release from the Federal Minister for the Environment and Heritage, Senator Robert Hill, identified Australia's grasslands as 'the Cinderella of environmental protection ... often overshadowed by more favoured environmental causes such as the protection of rainforests and coral reefs'.[7] The Minister was probably right when he said, 'I think it would surprise most Australians to know that the ecosystems that contain the most plant species threatened with extinction are native grasslands—not our tropical forests or our eucalypt forests.' In southern and southeastern Australia, less than 1 percent of the original 3.5 million hectares of grasslands remain in good condition.

This critical situation for the lower level understorey ecosystem is repeated internationally. In the UK, the area of lowland heath has decreased by 83 percent over the last century, while the picture for wild grasslands is even worse. Between 1930 and 1984 the area covered by natural grasslands declined by 97 percent. And although the value of these ecologies has now been recognised by the setting aside of reserves and a subsequent increase of grassland area, the species richness of Britain's wildflower meadows has continued to decline. The European story is similar, while in North America, more than 99 percent of the once great prairies are gone. It was here that the world's most extensive grassland once grew. Known as the Great Plains, it covered more than a quarter of continental US, parts of southern Canada and northern

Mexico. This vast and rich prairie extended eastward from the Rocky Mountains for more than 800 miles, and stretched over 3000 miles from north to south.

Pasture improvement and the trend away from mixed farming are the major causes of the loss of these deceptively simple-looking ecosystems. They also lack the obvious drama of the great forests on which much conservation attention has been focused.

One of my first jobs after graduating as a horticulturalist was on a grassland remnant in Hobart as part of a bush regeneration team. It is a dry, drab-looking hill known as the Domain, surrounded by highways, with commuters dashing to and from work around the base of this seemingly unimpressive lump of soil and rock. Meanwhile, above the cars and their preoccupied drivers, a miniature universe quietly goes about its existence, season after season. I was from a big city, and had never heard about grasslands before. For almost a year I spent my days roaming this soft world above the dull hum of the traffic. I had often been in tall forests, feeling small and hidden amongst the giants. In the grassland, I was the giant, each step of my boots crushing tiny wildflowers and their tiny insect companions. Part of my job was to make a plant collection. Day after day I wandered around, constantly discovering new plants, including a miniature orchid in flower. In spring the grasses bloom, becoming a rippling pastel ocean. Each autumn the seed heads turn the ocean to a glinting bronze. Exposed to the sun, the wind and the frost, the plants huddle down low, dominated by clumps of thin-leaved greyish grasses. I became entranced by the subtle and understated beauty of the place. It was a hidden beauty. You had to be down on your hands and knees to notice many of the flowers. You literally had to come down to its level, lie in the grass and look up close, like small children do.

We cannot hope to replicate the vast, lost grassland ecologies in our gardens, just as we cannot re-create forests. However, much potential understorey garden space is taken up by open areas in the form of lawn or flower beds, both of which are relatively high-need if well kept. In Australia, the severe droughts, water restrictions and introduction of user-pays water metering in recent years have been major factors in a national rethink about the place of the water-hungry exotic grasses that our lawns are based on. Concurrently, native grasses have surged in popularity and varieties selected for easy management and good appearance have come onto the market. Native grasses have become one of the 'lawn alternatives' which, like frog ponds, are now almost de rigueur in gardening manuals and as a segment theme used by the gardening media.

In reality, these things are not lawn alternatives, they are open-space alternatives. The list usually includes native grasses, groundcovers and herb lawns, all of which lack most of the qualities that make lawns attractive, functional and popular. They are not nice to sit on or play on (or not tough enough) and they usually lack the definition and colour contrast provided by a well-kept lawn. I suppose I prefer planting schemes to be chosen from a positive position that appreciates the special qualities of the selected plants, rather than as an alternative which feels like a worthy second choice because something else (lawns in this case) have lost favour in a politically correct world. Also, lawns are only an ecological disaster if they are *well-kept*.

The well-kept lawn is high need. It is a pampered pet, like a fussed-over, poison-dependent rose bush. The well-kept lawn, like the greens of the golf course in the catchment of my childhood lagoon, is indeed an ecological menace, dependent on high inputs of water, poison (I include artificial fertilisers under the poison banner) and fossil fuels. In search of just a small amount of incriminating evidence about the residual and run-off effects of pre-emergent herbicides, I embarked on a quick net surf. I soon found myself in the depths of a great swell and surge of American articles on lawn care. The more I read, the more I was gripped with horror. The amount of time and expense that Americans appear to put into poisoning their own front and back yards shocked me, even after all my years of exposure to horticultural sins.

One website (www.acehardware.com/info), belonging to a hardware shop with a vested interest in America's obsession with green uniformity as a symbol of civilisation and respectability, was particularly scary. Here's a run-down of some of their suggestions: initial applications of a pre-emergent herbicide; second-step applications with a post-emergent herbicide; follow-up applications for serious weed problems; spot treating with herbicides; killing 'insects that can do more damage to your lawn than you can possibly imagine'; as well as recommending products to control 'an abundance of lawn moss or diseases' or 'specifically designed to attack and kill common fungus problems'. Towards the end a little bit of advice appears which hints that the pre-emergent herbicide is not 100 percent benign: 'It is important that pre-emergent herbicide is watered in with about a quarter-inch of moisture. It is important not to overwater because the herbicide may easily run off with water into areas where it is not desired.'

Another US site, www.eartheasy.com, indicates that many Americans follow the hardware man's advice. It states that according to the

Environmental Protection Agency 'almost 80 million pounds of pesticide-active ingredients are used on US lawns annually'. Also astonishing are these statistics from the US National Wildlife Federation:

- 30 percent of water consumed on the US East Coast goes to watering lawns; 60 percent on the West Coast.
- The average suburban lawn receives 10 times as much chemical pesticide per acre as farmland.
- More than 70 million tons of fertilisers and pesticides are applied to residential lawns and gardens annually.
- A motorised lawnmower emits 10–12 times as much hydrocarbon as an average car; a brushcutter emits 21 times more; and a leaf blower 34 times more.
- Where pesticides are used on lawns, 60–90 percent of earthworms are killed.[8]

As a horticulture student I stopped eating apples following a lesson in which we were blandly informed of the fortnightly spray regime for apple orchards. After my lawn research, I no longer walk barefoot on smooth green grass.

But the future could be brighter. Another American says there is a way to have your lawn and walk on it too. Frank Bormann, in his book *Redesigning the American Lawn*, suggests that we should consider converting to what he calls a 'freedom lawn'. Knowing that freedom in all its forms is a core American value, I am hopeful that his ideas might be taken up en masse.

The freedom lawn is made up of a variety of plants, including clover and violets, as well as grasses. The diversity of plants helps the lawn to cope with stresses such as drought and disease so that no watering or spraying is needed. The result, freedom in many forms — freedom from expense, freedom from time spent in lawn care, and the freedom to play without being poisoned.

The description of Bormann's freedom lawn brings on déjà vu — surely he wrote the book after visiting Australia, as many people here already enjoy these freedoms (I know that I do), as their lawns go brown in summer drought, flower brightly with the yellows and whites of cats' ear, dandelion, clover and daisies and are fed by leaving the lawn clippings in situ. For areas where it is not practical to eliminate lawn altogether, the so-called 'freedom lawn' is a good way to go, as it reduces the ecological impact of having lawn. But it still does not *maximise* the garden's contribution to the environment. And that is our aim.

The lawn is an aspect of the understorey. My suggestion is to reduce to a minimum the amount of lawn you keep, and to 'freedom' manage the bit you retain. To do this effectively it is best if the lawn is made up of grasses chosen for their drought tolerance and suitability to your area. Some excellent research in recent years has focused on developing low-need turf grasses.

The rest of the areas that need to be kept open can become 'ex-lawn', rather than 'lawn alternative'. It is into this 'ex-lawn' that more understorey can go — a blend of shrubs, herbs, groundcovers and native grasses, depending on your site and aesthetic requirements. Innovative growers and nurseries have selected native grasses and strap-leafed plants for garden and public planting situations. These selections are worth looking for, maintaining good colour even in drought, and producing less straw. The reduction in straw is not only an advantage aesthetically, but also from the angle of fire-hazard reduction. Examples include *Poa labillardieri* 'Eskdale', *Elvera* (lavender grass), *Isolepis nodosa* 'Arida', *Lomandra longifolia* 'Katrinus' or 'Cassica', and *Themeda australis* 'Mingo'.

WILDFLOWER MEADOWS

Australia does not have meadows or fields. It has paddocks and grasslands. The tradition of meadow gardening is European. It is in France that perhaps the strongest revival of this form is occurring, with areas of abandoned agricultural land being converted into wildflower meadows, as well as small patches and drifts being created in gardens.

However, the idea of wildflower meadows can be transposed into the Australian garden. A wildflower meadow is a naturalistic carpet of mixed grasses and simple flowers, chiefly annuals, which can replace both lawn and flowerbeds. Such plantings are low-input, and hence low-maintenance. They exclude weeds and attract a multitude of insect life. In Australia, exotic wildflowers are mainly used as the seed for natives of this type is not readily available. Mixes of cosmos, poppies, sunflowers, alyssum, cornflower, calendula, marigold, coriander, nigella and lupins combine to paint a vibrant, romantic landscape. Australian flowers blended with native grasses can be used if a little effort is taken to source the seed. Many of the most suitable Australian wildflowers originate in Western Australia. The everlasting daisy is a good example of a wildflower perfectly suited to this style of gardening. The rule of thumb is to use simple, single flowers as they are hardy and attractive to wildlife.

Jerry Coleby-Williams, one-time head gardener of the Sydney Botanic Gardens, wrote about meadow gardening in the Summer 2000 issue of the *Organic Gardener* magazine, pointing out the biodiversity benefits with a picturesque description:

> *In casting the seeds for a meadow garden, gardeners will not only be wowed by their transient exuberance in flower, but will create al fresco restaurants, nightclubs, bed chambers and nurseries for an impromptu animal festival. Many of these visiting animals — birds, spiders, and insects — will benefit your garden, as they tend to control chewing and sap-sucking pests.*[9]

THICKETS, PRICKLES AND MESSY PLACES AS HOME

To meet the accommodation needs of garden wildlife, the understorey must be dense. A prickly tangle is a haven for many nesting birds — and vital protection. Scrubby thickets give protection from larger birds that may be nest predators, as well as the more obvious threats from cats and dogs. Dense, prickly shrubberies are not usually beloved of gardeners, as they can be messy and 'hard to manage'. In the environmental garden, however, mess and less management are often a good thing.

The Birds on Farms Survey explains with a note of frustration that 'a significant threat to farm birds and other wildlife is the impulse to "tidy up" the farm—clear that messy scrub patch or remove that fallen tree'.[10] It is in just these forgotten, unattended places that birds and other small creatures find food and shelter. Rotting logs and other debris harbour delightful and tasty communities of fungi, lichen, invertebrates, skinks and tiny frogs, perhaps, if it is damp. The role of rotting logs and debris as habitat and food is so important it rates as Guideline 8 in the recommendations made in the survey: 'Leave fallen trees to break down naturally.' [11]

The average garden obviously doesn't have fallen trees and scrub patches, but the point should be taken in context. Ground litter and thickets are vital for birds, and therefore for biodiversity in general. And, as we discuss in the next chapter, if the thicket is beside water, even better.

ON THE GROUND BELOW

Below the understorey is the ground itself. Ground-feeding birds scratch through the leaf litter searching for insects. Many reptiles, frogs and small native mammals as well as numerous invertebrates depend on the rich soil ecosystem that is found around rotting logs and leaf litter build-up. In the garden, this usually equates with a mulch layer, which is essential for a variety of gardening and environmental reasons.

You may not be able to have fallen trees and rotting logs, but there are other ways of generating similar conditions. The compost heap is an ecology in itself, a sort of festival of mini life forms, a quiet frenzy of birth, consumption and death contained in the piled-up debris of larger life forms. Boulders and rock piles, half-buried terracotta drain pipes, prunings left to decay in a back corner, even a wood pile or stack of bricks or roofing tiles left in the damp, dark back blocks of the smallest garden will be a cosy home for obscure, shy creatures of the dark zones, such as slaters, millipedes and their ilk.

The ground, after all, is the foundation of the whole garden metropolis. Life means health; below ground, at ground level and thence into the layers of vegetation that rise up, becoming what we see as 'garden'. By encouraging both soil life and ground level life, the plants we enjoy will be healthier. Their roots are part of the life in the soil.

The root zone is a quiet and complex place. It should be a busy place, teeming with the life and death of billions of bacteria, silken strands of fungal hyphae, the compact bodies of beetles, grubs, worms and crickets. The plants above depend on this world below. Create and allow conditions that favour life from under the ground to the tops of the tree canopy. Leave a bit of mess sometimes and let intricacy happen.

Mulch is vital. Clumping plants, ground cover plants, rocks, logs, moisture, privacy, places to hide, no poison — these simple things are the basis of the strategy for ground level and below. Stand back and try to imagine what you cannot see — the life that maintains your garden's foundation.

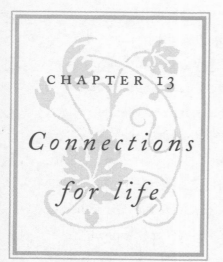

CHAPTER 13

Connections for life

A GARDEN IS MUCH MORE THAN A PLANTING SCHEME. Maximising the ecological value of a garden means looking at it from all angles. This happens of its own accord as your understanding of nature deepens. Other elements that attract life are water and the provision of specialised habitats such as nest boxes. Some people may also be interested in endangered species preservation. Knowing the way your plants, water and other special habitats connect and interact with the outside world is part of this understanding. Before moving on to these aspects of the ecological garden, let's take a closer look at the biodiversity of the plants themselves.

The issue of biodiversity loss on a global scale and the reasons for seeking ways of reversing this situation have already been discussed. As gardeners seek to play a role in maintaining the biodiversity of their region, considerations such as seedlings and species versus cloned cultivars and hybrids, and the provenance of the plants, arise.

Provenance means the place of origin. 'Purists' will only use plants grown from seed collected in local bush, if there is local bush. Paul Thompson's perspective as a designer and environmentalist is useful. In *Australian Planting Design* he writes:

There are two reasons for being concerned about provenance: the first is for the horticultural understanding and exploitation of variants, and the second is for the preservation of genetic diversity for scientific and conservation reasons. Sometimes there is conflict. There are increasing numbers of people who advocate only growing species collected from the local areas for reasons of preserving diversity. This objective is valid yet is not always practical or appealing to the broader population.[1]

The concept of biodiversity is about genetic diversity. This is lost when a plant selected for traits that suit humans — big, bright flowers, long, even flowering patterns, standardised shape, dwarfing habit — is mass produced for sale to the public. And as we have seen, there are times when these choices result in the exclusion or marginalisation of some species of birds, insects and other fauna. Having said that, there are times when a cultivar is the best choice. For example, a dwarf snow gum is available. In a garden unsuited to large trees, such selections mean trees can be planted where space is tight or there are limitations such as overhead power lines. Given the importance of plant layering — if habitat and foraging potential are to be maximised — the use of dwarf eucalypts in suburban Australia certainly has a place. Their flowers still provide nectar, their leaves can be nibbled on and sipped on just the same, the recluses of the wildlife world can still creep and crawl in the dark seclusion beneath the bark, in the wood, or amongst the roots.

One characteristic that ornamentals are often selected for is continuous or repeat flowering. If these flowers retain their nectar and pollen contents and are attractive and accessible to those that would feed from them, they are nature's equivalent of extended shopping hours. We are concerned here with areas in which the ecologies are impoverished and the land area covered by vegetation, especially complex vegetation, is severely reduced. In such circumstances, repeat flowering in the plants that *are* present is a great advantage to those who feed from the sweet cup of flowers. *Grevillea* 'Robyn Gordon' is an example.

Possibly the most popular and enduring Australian hybrid is *Grevillea* 'Robyn Gordon'. Originating in the renowned Myall Park Botanic Garden and created by Dave Gordon on his property in outback Queensland, its large, red flowers are virtually continuous. Birds and insects feast on the nectar that drips from the blooms. It is a hybrid that resulted from the planting together of a number of different *Grevillea* species in the 1960s. Registered with the Australian Cultivar Authority in 1973, this plant could be said to have paved the way for widespread acceptance of Australian plants as garden ornamentals. This contribution alone shows the value of garden selections in helping Australians make the cultural transition from gardens dominated by exotic plantings and style to ones which are born out of the Australian landscape.

Using seedlings means being prepared for a more uneven effect and possibly irregular and patchy flowering habits. Good planting design is of even greater importance in the creation of a beautiful and interesting garden based around seedlings of local species. Most amateur gardeners do not have this skill, yet they desire a garden that has aesthetic appeal and interest for as much of the year as possible. It is important that gardeners love their gardens and are inspired and satisfied by them. The brilliance of colour in the garden lifts our spirits, just as the softness of its greens soothes our minds. The inclusion of some cultivars and hybrids of native plants ensures colour and pleasing form, both of which help meet the aesthetic needs of garden owners who have previously branded Australian plants as boring and rough. From the point of view of the environment, better a hybrid grevillea than a double camellia.

Ultimately each gardener must choose the direction they take in plant selection. It is a matter of working with an understanding of the relationship between the environment and the garden, and from within this framework developing your garden according to personal inclinations. By understanding and working with what went before, in terms of soil, climate and plants, your garden needs you less and is easier to care for. This low-input garden can be very nearly self-sufficient in terms of energy, while having a positive interaction with the world beyond the boundaries. Growing some high-need plants like vegies can still be fitted into the overall garden plan in a way that is in line with the big-picture philosophy of ecological gardening, and this is looked at in the next chapter.

CREATING CONNECTIONS:
CORRIDORS AND PATCHES

All the good intention in the world does not change the fact that most birds and other wildlife need more than a garden-sized space for survival. While farmers can manage their properties to include sizable wildlife corridors and town planners can work to establish green belts in cities, the gardener has direct control only over their own small, seemingly isolated patch of land. However, this should not be a discouragement. The point has already been made that gardens join each other and their combined size is increasing and therefore increasingly significant. They also adjoin and occur in between parks, reserves, nature strips and roadside plantings. The planting of gardens for biodiversity must be seen as complementing the efforts of rural landholders and local government authorities, as well as having its own intrinsic value.

If some environmental gardens are isolated at the moment, they can still be ecological epicentres in their own right, stop-overs for travelling birds, and maybe in days to come, they will emerge as the mature ecology in a ribbon of younger ecologies when other gardeners come online as environmentalists.

Research into the value of small patches of planted native vegetation for biodiversity conservation is in its infancy. Ironically, the research itself depends on plantings that have been made because of the motivation and drive of individuals and groups to revegetate small areas without scientific proof that their projects will be effective. The Birds on Farms Survey is one such example. At a more official level, a report titled 'Assessing the Benefits of Vegetation Enhancement for Biodiversity: a draft framework' was written for Environment Australia in May 2003 by David Freudenberger and Judith Harvey. Its examination of 'patch scale' plantings is the closest it comes to the role gardens can play. Unable to make firm conclusions given the lack of available data, the report offers a number of 'insights'. Insights 1 and 2 are of particular relevance to our subject.

Insight 1 states that, 'Small-scale revegetation projects can provide occupiable habitat for a remarkable diversity of woodland and forest birds.' It goes on to say that mixed plantings of native trees and shrubs are providing homes 'for some birds which are showing regional declines in eastern and southern Australia'.[2]

Insight 2 places the patches into a broader context, both geographi-cally, and in time. It states that, 'The habitat values of revegetation will change with time and are dependent on broader landscape characteristics.' Elaborating on this point, it also says 'the habitat values of the revegetation will change for centuries, as today's seedlings eventually grow old enough to support hollows for the wide range of hollow-dependent vertebrates and invertebrates'. This means that the 'small and isolated patches of revegetation' that exist today may ultimately become 'centres in a connected network of corridors and enlarged remnants, as the slow but cumulative effects of small individual efforts merge into significantly altered landscape patterns'.[3]

The importance of the combined efforts of individuals and groups involved in revegetation on various scales is recognised by the report which says, 'The past 20 years of vegetation enhancement activities are beginning to show what is possible.' Interestingly, it is at the patch-scale level that 'some positive responses are being detected' and 'some attributes of biodiversity are responding to vegetation enhancement in a way desired by a wide range of interested people'.[4]

While reports such as this are required by policy-makers responsible for allocating budget to thousands of community-based projects around Australia, it is the communities themselves that are determining the nature of the projects, and thousands of hours of voluntary time do not appear in the reckoning statements at government level. The contribution made by gardeners is even more invisible. The environmental project you undertake in your own garden is 100 percent funded by you and is unlikely to be part of any biodiversity assessment study. Such is your freedom to make a difference in your own way and without accountability! You can rest assured that the birds and butterflies and blue tongues don't read the reports and survey maps. They will come where they are made welcome, their existence providing material for future surveys.

The bigger the life-friendly area the better, but the combined area of many small gardens is important, especially if they are adjacent to each other. There may also be others around you who are trying to develop habitat/ecological gardens, and your garden will relate to those gardens, multiplying the effect of each one. My neighbours and I each have blocks of about 1000 square metres. At least four of us in a row and one below me are planting local species, with no particular coordination or communication about this, beyond some plant sharing and occasional conversations. So, the area across which local plants are being used is 5000 square metres, not just 1000.

As a gardener you basically work alone. Yet the surveys (and common sense) show that when the aim is to attract nature, the position of the garden in relation to other habitats can be as important as the design of the garden itself. A garden may be an isolated habitat, as is an oasis in the desert or an island in the sea; it may be a stepping stone between habitats or it may form part of a greenbelt, or corridor, if neighbouring gardens and open spaces are also planted as refuges. Depending on the garden size and the needs of species, a garden may even be a viable habitat in its own right. This can certainly be true for invertebrates, which are vital links in the biodiversity web.

To illustrate the value of *all* patches of nature-welcoming land, insight can be gleaned from taking a closer look at the lifestyle of our travelling birds. As many as 40 percent of Australia's woodland birds are migratory to some degree, while 80 percent of Australia's 73 species of honeyeaters are nomadic. To highlight the richness of this country's biodiversity (remembering also that birds are a biodiversity indicator), consider that worldwide there are 151 species of honeyeater—that means that here in the driest continent we have almost half the world's honeyeater species.

People have become the dominators and determiners of the shape of much of the landscape. This dominance brings with it a responsibility to consider and take care of the inhabitants of that landscape. In the human context it is called 'duty of care'. We can aim to extend that duty of care to the travelling birds that follow the nectar flows of the *eucalypts*, *banksias*, *melaleucas*, *grevilleas* and other native plants as they bloom across the seasons. Birds prefer to fly along strips of native vegetation rather than cross open areas. Each dash across a treeless zone is a risk. Therefore, each patch of native vegetation is a potential life saver. Gardeners have the power to create these stepping stones, effectively pit-stops for travelling birds. If they link to other plantings, so much the better. If these gardens do not exist in the first place, there is no chance for the links to connect.

The garden's planting design creates its foundation as a habitat or stop-over. But first-class accommodation attracts repeat visitors by offering more than the basics. Whether in one's hometown or on the road, we all know that it is over drinks that you meet the most diverse range of characters, of whatever species.

WATER MEANS LIFE

Research has shown that a *reliable* source of clean water is the single most important factor in attracting and keeping birds in gardens. Using birds as a biodiversity indicator, it can be assumed that overall biodiversity goes up when there is a water supply such as a pond or birdbath. Birdbaths provide drinking and splashing water, but a pond meets a wider range of needs. As mentioned above, it is ideal if the prickly thicket is beside water. For some birds and other creatures the cooler, moister habitat that can be created around water is essential. For others, the shrubs beside the water offer a safe bolt-hole from the pond edge if danger threatens while they are drinking or preening. The combination of water, flowers and humidity also brings more insects, which, of course, attract more birds. For frogs, water is an obvious must, and lizards will come both for a drink and easy insect pickings.

Providing water helps maximise the potential of your own plot. In this way you create opportunities for other life forms. Let me tell you about a dragonfly I was once surprised by.

I used to work for *Gardening Australia*, a gardening television program and magazine, which Australian gardeners will know well. Each year in Sydney we staged a four-day gardening expo, *Gardening Australia Live*. During this time display gardens were built, viewed and dismantled. I spent the four days on site, walking many miles no doubt, as I kept tabs on my various duties. I recall a quick moment as I strolled past an outside display garden that included a minimalist, designer-style water feature. I saw a dragonfly, darting in its hyperactive way about the surface of that ever-so-temporary and clinical pond. Somehow that water-seeker had found the small body of water, within those few days and in a location of concrete and asphalt. I chanced upon it at that very moment. No doubt there were other such visitors without tickets that I did not see. Such creatures are great travellers. Small birds migrate vast distances. Who are we to say what role a small patch of life-friendly garden may have in sustaining some link in the ecological chain? What we do know is that if provision is not made to sustain these links, the chain disintegrates.

Unlike the transitory pond at the gardening expo, your garden's water supply MUST be reliable. Birds will come to depend upon it, and on a hot summer's day, if the water has all dried up, a small thirsty bird might also dry up. The smaller the body of water, the more vulnerable it is to the thirst of sun and wind. Birdbaths are small, and often they are highly exposed, as they double as garden ornaments or features. Here are some guidelines for making birdbaths bird-friendly. Ensure:

- Clean, shallow water, so that birds can safely preen and splash in it.
- Non-slip surfaces, so that they can easily perch on and grip the edge.
- Thick plant cover nearby for safety, or else they may not risk a drink in the first place.
- An overhanging perch.
- Protection from cats—a birdbath hanging from tree branches is a good idea.
- Shade from the heat of midday and afternoon sun.

There are also ponds and ponds. Optimise the nature-friendliness of your pond by including as many of the following as possible:

- Shallow and/or boggy edges.
- A rock or island—a floating island, or a large potted water plant placed in the centre, can be used in smaller ponds.
- Overhanging rocks or logs around the edge for fish, tadpoles and other small, vulnerable things to shelter and hide under.
- A variety of depths so that pond dwellers can escape from heat and predators.

- Dense shrubs and/or reeds along the edges for refuge and food supply.
- Some overhanging vegetation.
- Afternoon shade to keep it all cool.
- Morning sun to warm it all up.
- Something for perching on— the overhanging vegetation might meet this need.
- Water plants for hiding in, feeding on and in, and to help keep the water clean.

SPECIALISED HOMES

Just like humans, some critters are fussier about the size, shape and position of their abode than others. It is these particular animals that are likely to be more in need of our help for their survival, as they are less adaptable to a changing environment and therefore more vulnerable to habitat loss. Quite often these creatures have had a limited distribution in the first place, perhaps because of their specific nesting and/or feeding needs.

The particular nesting habits of some birds come to mind. Food needs are more likely to be met incidentally— by that I mean that if you simply plant a range of locally occurring flowering and fruit/seed-bearing trees, shrubs and grasses, plus have a pond, you are likely to cover most bases. If the birds are insect eaters, then this same broad approach will attract the insects that attract the birds. For nesting, however, some of the very specific requirements take considerable effort to create. You cannot do this unless you know which species from your area have these needs, and what the needs are. If your aim is to maximise the garden's ecological potential, some detailed knowledge of the fauna that is natural to the area is essential. Research may tell you that the habitat needs of an increasingly rare creature can be created in your own backyard.

However, taking environmental gardening in the direction of endangered species preservation takes the project to another level and is not for everyone. You need to become more of a specialist, and have the time to focus on developing the garden in this way. I have not gardened in this way myself, and would advise those who are interested to make contact with biologists and ecologists working locally on rare-species preservation. It is important work, and the increased biodiversity resulting in your garden will bring both greater stability and dynamism to the overall ecosystem. To make the most positive contribution, it is best to join forces with others working in the area of species preservation. Species facing extinction are often fussy, you could say idiosyncratic. To help them, you must get to know them.

The red-tailed black cockatoo is one such individual in need of personal case management. These large, flamboyant birds make a dramatic and sky-filling squawk as they fly in flocks or small groups, their wide, strong wings slowly pumping the air. Gazing up at the black shapes against the great pale sky, Australians mutter that rain must be coming. If perchance you live in the southern part of the Victorian/South Australian border and you are researching the local fauna that might come to your garden, your research will tell you that an original inhabitant of your area is a sub-species of the red-tailed black cockatoo. You will also find out that the destruction of both its food source — brown stringy-bark forests — and its nesting sites — the hollows of dead red gums — are making it hard for this bird to maintain its population. At the time of writing, the population is estimated at 500 to 1000.

Wanting to support these birds' simple quest to live, you might make the effort to install nest boxes that meet their needs, and if you have space, plant a brown stringy-bark or two. As you made your enquiries you would find out that Birds Australia are working with the community to help this bird both by campaigning for the preservation of old red gums and by providing nest boxes to landowners.

Depending on where you live, it may also be possible to encourage arboreal mammals, such as gliders, bats, possums and even koalas. As with birds, some information on who might have lived on your land before it was developed will enable you to provide for their needs, and thus make it possible for them to move back in. Many of these creatures depend on hollows in trees, so nesting boxes can be a useful substitute. However, the creation of artificial nest sites should be approached with caution. Such homes must be well constructed, positioned securely at the correct height and then kept an eye on in case unwanted species take up residence. The Gould League's *The Nest Box Book* says that, 'Unless adequately planned, nest box installation has potential to damage rather than help native species. Installation is only a first step. Management is vital for success.'[5]

The same principles apply to other fauna such as frogs and reptiles.

THE PATH TO BIODIVERSITY

The whole is greater than the sum of the parts. The ecosystem garden is living, breathing proof of this truism. If you recognise and nurture the different elements within the garden as habitat for other life forms, they will come. If you respect the separate ecosystems of the soil, mulch layer, groundcovers, lawns, water, shrubberies, the bark of each tree, each individual flower, the compost heap, the messy corners, the wood heap, the cracks between pavers, the cool, damp, shadowy places, the underside of a leaf, then each of these will interact and develop in their own way, as the dynamic of life continues with its living and dying, simply because you allow it to. Each of these, from the single leaf to the complex universe within a compost heap, support aspects of life that are often unseen, and in a garden that is free of poisons and where intervention is minimised, these life-support systems will flourish. The quiet world of micro-organisms, the bizarre universe of insects and other arthropods, the delightful presence of birds, the quaintness of wide-eyed frogs, the rustle of skittering lizards, and the surprise of other uninvited guests, wanted and unwanted, will animate your habitat garden when you create conditions that allow the structural elements of the garden to work and interact together as only they know how.

Think of yourself as a conductor. The starting point is to have a feeling for the garden as a whole, as a blended work of nature, in the way that a conductor understands and feels the sound and emotion and beauty of the whole symphony. Have a glimpse of the whole, like an insight into something that cannot be fully grasped. Then aim to manage the individual components in a way that allows them to network with their neighbours, to do team work that is life-friendly and life-rich. Just as the best conductors create the possibility of each musician playing with greater depth and intensity, so you create the possibility of the garden becoming a richer, more vibrant community of life.

In summary, here are the strategies you can use to maximise the biodiversity of your garden:

- **Use a range of plants that provide nectar, pollen, fruit and**

seeds —Planting local species will ensure that local fauna are
adapted to the flowers and fruits without you having to know too
much about this. Repetition and diversity are both important,
ecologically and aesthetically. This can be achieved by planting
groups of each species in a pattern throughout the garden or bed.

• **Plant in layers** — Ensure that there are trees, shrubs and ground
plants to meet the needs of the widest possible range of fauna.
In this way you can provide for critters that feed in the bark of
trees and the mulch on the ground, as well as the more obvious
flower, leaf and fruit feeders. Height is important, and so too is
understorey. Meeting these needs can be combined with design
sensitivity to create a beautiful garden, just as nature creates
a beautiful landscape.

• **Use no poisons**—Poisons are just that. It is virtually impossible
to affect only the target organism when using poison. The thing
you are targeting, whether insect, fungus or bacteria, is the food
of another life form. When you kill with poison, several flow-on
effects are possible: other creatures are killed directly by the
application, perhaps by spray drift or by direct hit; other creatures
are killed or weakened by eating the poisoned organism; other
creatures go hungry because the poisoned organism was their
food source; and the poison makes its way into the soil where it
may be residual in its original form or where it may be broken
down into other chemicals — whichever it is, these residues can
be long lasting, they can reduce the life in your soil, make their
way gradually into water courses, and remain in the food chain
where their ultimate effects are not fully understood, even today.

- **Tolerate some damage to plants from insects and diseases**—
  Some creatures are leaf feeders, others are flower feeders while
  yet others nibble on fruits, seeds, bark or even wood. The
  perfection of nature lies in its multitude of imperfections,
  as the constant stream of interaction is the melting pot of
  existence. Nature loves usefulness. It loves dynamism and activity
  and change and survival. Nature is in a constant state of
  transformation. There is no stasis. The caterpillar eats the leaf.
  The caterpillar is food for the bird or is parasitised by bacteria.
  The caterpillar that survives becomes a butterfly. The butterfly
  sips nectar and transfers pollen and is food for another bird.
  All these depend on the leaf being eaten. When you have
  a balance, there will not be too much damage. Tolerate a little
  more damage at the outset as a balance is established. Remember
  my peach aphids and ladybirds. I could have hosed off the aphids,
  or sprayed them with garlic or pyrethrum. But then I would not
  have allowed the ladybirds to move in. Instead of seeing a chewed
  flower bud as having been ruined, shift your mind and you will
  instead see the birds and butterflies that have been given life by
  the caterpillar that chewed the precious bud. The bud *is*
  precious— whether as a meal or as the form preceding a flower
  that opens as perfectly as you have hoped.
- **Have a pond or permanent water source** — Ponds bring insects,
  birds, reptiles, amphibians and mammals. All life needs water.
  The role of ponds in the food chain is many-fold. It supplies food
  directly to things that live in it, such as tadpoles, frogs and
  water-based insects. Secondly, the pond attracts many other life

forms as visitors, and these feed on each other as well as on the pond life itself. For example, birds and lizards will come to feed on the multitude of insect life which is drawn to the pond. And, of course, it should go without saying that everyone needs a drink as well as food, and this is why they often come in the first place. A pond or water supply has been shown to be the single most important factor in keeping a population of birds in a garden.

• **Provide shelter, nesting sites and materials** — The provision of shelter and breeding locations also requires a blend of plant selection and structural design. The same principles of planting apply as for food. In terms of shelter and nesting for birds, frogs, lizards and mammals, it must be emphasised that dense shrub and groundcover layers are vital. For the birds this includes a prickly shrubbery, for frogs it means using some broad-leafed and some clumping and strap-leafed vegetation, especially around the pond. Insects also have shelter needs in terms of vegetation and again, the structure of the planting is important. The needs of many organisms are subtle and go unnoticed by us. Temperature, humidity, light intensity and wind strength are all factors that can make or break the viability of an insect or other faunal population. Nature is our best guide, so observe, observe, observe and then copy, copy, copy. Even better is the retention of clumps of natural vegetation, but for most of us this option is too late.

HIGH-NEED PLANTS ARE THE ONES THAT TAKE A LOT OF input and care, and though they may give much to the gardener in terms of satisfaction, joy and productivity, they give little back to the environment. Their needs are for food, water and protection from climate, pests and diseases. I include fruit and vegetables in this category, well-kept lawns and many exotic ornamentals. Organically grown fruit and vegies, however, *do* fit into the environmental garden. Home-grown food reduces cost to the environment in

terms of the transport and infrastructure needed in commercial production, as well as more directly by being organic and grown by hand, rather than broad-acre and grown by machine. The many other benefits and delights of home-grown organic food are well known.

High-need ornamentals are grown for different reasons. Many people simply see beautiful plants in nurseries or magazines and want to have them. We live in a consumer culture that promotes gratification. If we want something, we feel that we should be able to have it. Advice from nurseries and magazines about how to grow the gorgeous flowers we want usually involves buying more products — fertilisers, peat moss, sprays, irrigation, water crystals, pruning tools, books and so on. This approach to gardening is fraught with frustration and expense, both financial and environmental. The plants rarely perform as well as the ones in the pictures, and when the initial enthusiasm has worn off, the TLC also drops away. The plants struggle on, often looking sickly, leggy and not at all like the soft-focus image in the magazine that was so attractive in the first place. Azaleas, camellias, orchids, roses and fruit trees are commonly seen in this condition, with yellowed leaves, spider mite, black spot, scale, rotting buds and other signs of what we call 'neglect'. They only suffer from 'neglect', however, because in this environment they are high-need in the first place.

Those with a natural passion for plants and gardens often enjoy the challenge of growing 'difficult' plants. This is a different culture to the one described above. These are the gardeners who *do* look after their high-need plants. They love looking after them, and the results are stunning fruits, vegetables, flowers and gardens to be proud of. However, the fact remains that if a garden is dominated by high-need plants, the environmental audit sheet will not look good. Those who love to grow these plants but want to garden ecologically are rethinking their gardening style because of their values.

If some high-need ornamentals are to be grown, you can reduce their negative environmental impact in the following ways:

- Minimise their number — be selective and grow only the ones that most interest and attract you.
- Choose species, cultivars or hybrids suited to your soil and climate.
- Grow them organically.
- Zone them.

Zoning means to grow plants with the same or similar needs together, rather than scattering them all over the garden. Here are some guidelines for zoning in an environmental garden:

- Choose the part of the garden that best suits the plants in the first place, in terms of soil and climate needs.
- Prepare and maintain the soil according to organic soil improvement methods. This will ensure a good structure that retains water and nutrients and also releases them easily to plant roots. This means less top-up watering and feeding are needed, and stronger plants that are better equipped to resist pest and disease attack. It also means less nutrient and soil runoff. I include mulching in soil maintenance.
- Install efficient irrigation. This means only the area that needs water is irrigated; the timing and amount of water are regulated according to the needs of the plants; watering is done in the early morning, evening or at night to minimise evaporation.
- The zone might be restricted to or include potted plants. Potted plants can be managed for very specific needs without affecting the whole garden ecology.

FOOD CROPS IN THE ENVIRONMENTAL GARDEN

Much has been said about the importance of growing indigenous plants. Few of our food crops are Australian, let alone local to our own region. Although bush tucker has attracted much interest in the last 20 years or so, macadamia nuts remain the only important commercial food crop of Australian origin, and even their part in our diet is small.

Food growing is undeniably relevant to environmental gardens. There is much excellent literature available about growing food organically;

however, just as it is vital to grow local plants, I encourage you whenever possible to seek out books and magazines that are written for your local conditions. As I have mentioned, the publishing trend is towards globalisation. The value of a book written for your own area only really becomes apparent when you have one, and they are few and far between. You may have to settle for themed material, such as warm-climate gardening. Tasmania is once again lucky in this department, as its tradition of attracting and nourishing organic-gardening and food-growing wisdom continues.

The American gardening author and seedsman Steve Solomon settled in northern Tasmania some years ago and has self-published the book that every vegetable gardener dreams of. *Growing Vegetables South of Australia* is written for Tasmanian conditions, recommending varieties, planting times and gardening methods suited to this remote, and often left-off-the-map, island state.

He discusses the concept of bioregions in relation to gardening and plant selection. This approach adds a useful dimension to the idea of working with local information and plant material. The use of 'local' plants is recommended because of their suitability to local conditions and their interactions with local fauna. In the context of our exotic food crops we should still aim to choose varieties that suit local conditions. An understanding of bioregions extends our scope in this endeavour, and introduces reasons for making the effort to source propagation material from similar bioregions.

BIOREGIONS

Bioregions may be continents apart. They are areas with similar climatic conditions and perhaps latitudes. Steve Solomon came from Oregon where he founded a vegetable seed company based on supplying the local area only. In fact, he would refuse to send seed to customers from too far away, as he couldn't guarantee its performance out of his own area. He describes the climate of Oregon as being 'almost a mirror image of Tasmania's'.[1] The latitudes (one north and one south) are practically identical and the weather systems come in from the ocean, creating maritime climates in both places. Vegetable varieties that grow well in Oregon are likely to do well in Tasmania. Based on this reasoning, Solomon suggests that it makes more sense for Tasmanians to purchase seed that has been trialled and grown in the Pacific North-West of North America or in the UK than from mainland Australian seed companies where conditions are more than likely vastly different. It is a point not often made, particularly in an era when 'doing the right thing' includes buying Australian product. A more grassroots solution to the understanding that there are regional adaptations in vegetable varieties is involvement in seed-saving groups and networks. To this end, Solomon and others have established an online seed exchange where individuals can offer seed from their garden for sale.[2]

The vegetable gardening dilemma of which varieties to use and where to source seed are but one of the trickle-downs from the much bigger picture that has emerged from the commodification and monopolisation of the food-crop gene pool as agriculture has evolved into agribusiness. This has been discussed to some degree in *Chapter 10 — Fears for our food* in relation to trends that have stimulated the development of the culture of organic gardening and farming. But what does it all mean for life in your own backyard and the decisions you need to make? Some background into the relationship between agricultural plants and humans brings a depth of understanding to this issue, which involves both science and culture.

Just as wild plants have special adaptations to their native region, so too do the domestic plants that have been cultivated for many hundreds or even thousands of years. In the case of our food plants, however, there is also a direct and intrinsic relationship with people, the cultivators. The relationship between these plants and their people, or these people and their plants, is virtually symbiotic. David Suzuki puts it most gracefully in his book *Wisdom of the Elders*:

> *Perhaps nowhere is the unwritten pact between humans and plants more explicit than between farmers and their domesticated crops. Often genetically modified to the point of utter dependency upon their human caretakers for survival, wheat, corn, and other agricultural plant species now share our own biological destiny. Their evolutionary fates have become inextricably intertangled with our own.*[3]

How plants and humans reached this state is the story of agriculture itself. For most of its history agriculture was based around a small local economy. Each valley or ridge grew the varieties of wheat, rice, maize or potatoes that had been selected by farmers for their ability to thrive in that particular valley or on that particular ridge. Across millennia and across the globe, peasant farmers and gardeners saved seed from their harvest for the sowing of the next season's crop. Obviously, they saved the seed of the best performers, both in terms of ease of growing and for culinary qualities. These simple people, often the poorest within their society, held in their rustic storerooms a treasure trove of genetic diversity the like of which plant breeders and genetic engineers of the 21st century, with billions of dollars at their disposal, can only dream.

Each farmer, each village, each valley, from Ethiopia to Greece to China to the Andes, grew unique genetic strains of the foods that are our staples. Wheat, rice, maize, potatoes, barley, pulses, vegetables and fruit were grown from season to season, from year to year, from century to century, continually adapting to and being selected for, the conditions peculiar to each locality.

Regions of extreme plant diversity, both in natural and agricultural ecosystems, developed in areas where the climate and topography meant that life continued to flourish and diversify while the temperate zones were in the grip of the ice age. These places are known as the Vavilov Centres, after the Russian botanist who identified them. Other than the Mediterranean, the Vavilov Centres are all in the Third World. In modern times, however, the combined pressures of world trade, agribusiness and foreign debt have pushed the peasant farmers of these areas, their traditions and their seed stock to virtual extinction. The world's food supplies depend on the Vavilov Centres for genetic material, but the world food industry is wiping them out.

Remnants are all that is left of the gardening and farming traditions that kept these food crops and the people that grew them alive for so long. The story of the food stuffs we take for granted is becoming lost knowledge, just as the methods used to build the Sphinx and Stonehenge are a mystery to us in spite of the sophistication of modern engineering.

The arrogance of the mindset that labels the peasants and their traditions 'dispensable' is expressed in the belief that plant biodiversity can be preserved in gene banks. The fact that these institutions are generally under-funded and may be vulnerable to political instability exposes the whole arrangement as even more bizarre. The frailty of this system was shown in 1991 when civil war threatened Ethiopia's capital, Addis Ababa. A dramatic rescue of the seedbank was organised at the last minute by a group of scientists and activists meeting in Stockholm. The airlift involved the UN and the Dutch, Swedish and US governments. The only person missing, it seems, was James Bond.

Genetic diversity by its very nature is dynamic, vital and interactive. The relationship between the gentle traditions that nurtured food plant biodiversity and the crops themselves was symbiotic. Each depended on the other for survival. People existed within nature, participating in the evolution of the environment in which they lived, just as all animals do. It is indeed hard to see how the sterility of the gene bank can adequately replace these living, breathing systems. They are a solution developed by bureaucrats and laboratory-based scientists rather than food growers themselves. Somewhere along the way, commonsense was left behind.

Perhaps, in our obsession with the exciting world of science and technology, we have been blinded by our own brilliance. The adrenalin rush of genetic engineering has proved irresistible, although as we have seen, it may be doomed to marginalisation at the consumer level where commonsense still stands a chance. Yet the interminable sowing and growing and saving of seed cannot compete with Dolly the sheep or the Terminator gene as news stories. Farming and gardening are not exactly spectator sports — eking out an existence for thousands of years on the side of a mountain at high altitude has never been the stuff of headline news. So, while much excitement surrounds sporting events and Olympic record-breaking, the loss of a multitude of wheat, rice and vegetable species and the human culture and expertise that created them does not capture the imagination of the average newsmaker. I recall a conversation about organics with Senator Bob Brown, leader of the Australian Greens. Typically, he cut straight to an angle on organics that is seldom mentioned. While the organic movement is chiefly concerned with conversion of modern agriculture to organics, Bob's vision, ever that of a conservationist, saw the importance of *preserving* the organic agriculture that already exists. He was referring to the natural farming of peasant communities around the world which is basically ignored by the organic farming and gardening movement. Replacement is always harder and less efficient than preservation. This applies to organic food production just as it does to the efforts to revegetate degraded landscapes.

Things that are not valued become lost. We are in the midst of an extinction crisis that does not just mean the loss of a few obscure frog species and some oddball plants that never did very well anyway. It includes the ancestors of the food plants we depend on, leaving a swelling global population increasingly vulnerable to potato famine scenarios and dependant on expensive and toxic chemical solutions for crop protection. The irony is that although we often regard ourselves as the pinnacle of evolution, humans generally seem to place little value on all the small bits that make up the big picture of the survival jigsaw.

It is to the gene pools cultivated by the peasant farmers that modern plant breeders look for genes that give very specific qualities, such as resistance to a particular fungus, or wind hardiness. The internationalisation of the agricultural seed trade has reduced this incredible genetic heritage of crop diversity quite dramatically — to the point where, for example, if a gene is suddenly needed to combat the ravages of a pest there is a good chance that the gene has become extinct. The implications for farmers, particularly subsistence farmers, whose livelihoods depend on the success of each crop, is devastating when a weather event or pest outbreak — that a traditional variety would have survived — decimates the expensive, 'high-producing' hybrid crop which lacks such precise adaptation to the locale. Its high-productivity potential becomes irrelevant when an unusually strong wind flattens its long green stalks, and it barely produces at all. That is another story, although it has relevance to gardeners who grow their own food.

Community-based seed networks and exchanges use this same principle of local adaptation in their preference for vegetable and fruit varieties with a proven track record in their own locality. By making a little extra effort to source such seed, you make your life as a gardener easier. There will be fewer failures and disappointments as well as less time and expense in crop protection. Also, the environmental impact will be less, as inputs reduce.

Collecting seed from the best performers in your own garden brings this approach to its logical conclusion. Evolution is everywhere, not just in science books. As long as you grow species plants, they will each be genetically unique. Those that grow best in your garden will have some slight genetic variation that predisposes them to the conditions they have experienced in that growth cycle. Those conditions will vary from season to season. Hence the wisdom in continuity of a seed line for a particular area. From season to season, different conditions will favour different gene combinations. The astute seed-saver selects individual plants for a range of desirable characteristics. Over time, through cross-pollination, this range of characteristics may increasingly be seen in combination in individual plants.

PLANT PROTECTION PRIORITIES

Gardening organically often assumes and advises the use of various concoctions made from plant-derived poisons or other deterrents or interrupters of lifecycles.

Pyrethrum is the most important of the plant-derived poisons to be commercialised. It originates from a small white daisy, *Chrysanthemum cinerariaefolium*. Perhaps the greatest advantage of pyrethrum as an insecticide is its biodegradability. This means it breaks down quickly, leaving no toxic residue. It is highly vulnerable to light, so must be used fresh and is only effective for a short time. Another advantage is that it's not toxic to mammals. However, pyrethrum is a broad-spectrum contact insecticide. That is, it kills a wide range of insects on contact. That includes the so-called beneficials, the predators and pollinators, with the exception of bees. It is relatively ineffective against larvae, but is toxic to fish. Rotenone, or derris, is another plant-derived poison which is highly biodegradable. It kills a range of crop pests and is also deadly to fish. Rotenone has some toxicity to mammals, although this seems to be quite variable from species to species. Children are known to be sensitive to it, and human fatalities, though rare, can occur.

There are two concerns in the way that these and other 'organic' pesticides are used and promoted. One is that they are often marketed and handled as though they are completely benign. They are not. The poisoners of ancient Rome knew well the toxic qualities of many plants. The other concern is that these products are usually non-selective. If a lacewing or ladybird is feeding on the aphids when you spray pyrethrum, they will die, along with the sap-suckers. Under these conditions, a balanced garden ecology will still have trouble establishing itself, in spite of organic credentials and good intentions. Also, unless there is some pest build up, the predators do not have the chance to build up their population to numbers that can effectively deal with the problem.

Integrated Pest Management, known as IPM, includes the use of pyrethrum and other non-residual pesticides. IPM is often put forward as the ideal in pest management, and certainly it is a vastly more intelligent approach than simply following a spray routine as recommended by pesticide manufacturers. IPM takes a bigger-picture, more careful approach to pest management. It considers the factors such as pest life cycles, damage thresholds, use of pest and disease resistant varieties and environmental care. A key aspect of IPM is to monitor pest build-up so that spraying is only used when there is a threat to commercial levels of production. The preferred sprays are selective (killing only the target species) rather than broad-spectrum, and non-residual in the environment. The advantages of this system over routine spraying are many. For one thing, it is much cheaper. Also, there is less human and environmental exposure to sprays and less opportunity for resistance to develop in the pest population. This is a simplified picture of IPM. We do not need great detail on this system here. Its development is a major step in the right direction for commercial agriculture, and many of its principles can be adopted by home gardeners. However, it is designed for large-scale production systems which are mainly monocultures based around the needs of agricultural machinery and a market that demands flawless produce. The aims of environmental gardening and food production are not fully met by IPM, particularly in the home garden where the pressure to produce a certain quantity and quality do not exist.

Pest and disease problems vary from area to area. The starting point for the environmental gardener is to manage the whole garden for ecological balance as a top priority. Once such a system is in place, there is very little need for spraying of any kind and it should always be a last resort. The only thing I occasionally spray for these days is peach leaf curl, a fungal disease readily controlled with an organically acceptable fungicide if the application is timed correctly. Snails and slugs often make seedling establishment difficult and use of low-toxicity, non-residual baits is preferable to repeatedly losing seedlings, although this should be a last resort if barrier and trapping methods fail. Be aware that birds and lizards may eat the poisoned bodies of the snails and slugs. However, if you don't grow the vegies yourself, you will have to buy them and the way they are grown is likely to have taken much more toll on the environment than a low-toxicity solution that is acceptable within the organic framework.

To minimise the need for invasive management of pests and disease, follow these gardening principles:

- Use organic methods to develop and maintain the foundation of a strong garden—a healthy, living soil. This includes ensuring that the soil is well drained by installing drainage or raising beds if waterlogging is a problem.
- Grow varieties suited to your climatic bioregion.

- Whenever possible, grow varieties with natural resistance to the pests and diseases that occur where you live.
- Avoid monocultures and practice crop rotation to prevent disease build-up in the soil. Crop rotation also helps maintain soil health by varying the depth of the root zone and varying the nutritional demands made on the soil.
- Include herbs and flowers in the vegetable growing area, both for companion-planting effects and to attract beneficial insects that may be nectar feeders.
- Minimise the amount of stress that plants experience. Like us, they are vulnerable and prone to attack and infection when in a weakened state. This includes growing them during the appropriate season and keeping up with their food and water needs.
- Manage the whole garden for biodiversity and ecological stability. This will ensure healthy populations of predatory birds, lizards, frogs and arthropods including spiders.
- Practice garden hygiene to minimise disease spread through pruning tools, rotting fruit and stagnant soils or potting mixes.

To sum up, the approach to food gardening is basically as for the rest of the garden:
- Choose plants suited to local conditions.
- Manage plants for minimal negative environmental impact (e.g. nutrient run-off, water wastage, spraying of poisons even if they are 'natural').
- Encourage biodiversity.

The romance with gorgeous, highly bred and exotic plants has to shift if the gardener is sincere in wanting to support the regional ecology. I do not advocate a purist approach: the inspiration and delight that the world's most beautiful trees and flowers bring are intrinsic to the experience and love of gardening. Each year when my oriental lily opens bloom after bloom of pure white fragrance, I believe in heaven on earth. The lily lives in a pot on my deck. My Mr Lincoln and Mothers' Love roses were gifts from special people and remind me of them. Connections like these are another layer in the meaning of gardens and should remain so. However, if you have a strong sense of environmental values, let the overall structure and content of the garden reflect that. Part of this is limiting the number of high-need plants and managing them wisely.

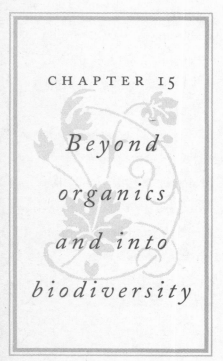

CHAPTER 15

Beyond organics and into biodiversity

IN 1962 RACHEL CARSON WROTE: 'IN SOME QUARTERS nowadays it is fashionable to dismiss the balance of nature as a state of affairs that prevailed in an earlier, simpler world — a state that has now been thoroughly upset and that we might as well forget it … The balance of nature is not the same today as in Pleistocene times, but it is still there: a complex, precise, and highly integrated system of relationships between living things which cannot safely be ignored any more than the law of gravity can be defied by a man perched on the edge of a cliff. The balance of nature is not a *status quo*; it is fluid, ever shifting, in a constant state of adjustment. Man, too, is part of this balance'.[1]

The dynamism and fluidity of nature that Rachel Carson describes presents us with both challenges and opportunities. We can never know it all, regardless of ceaseless studies and analysis and scientific advances, for even as we make our studies, the picture is changing. A study of an ecosystem basically tells us about the organisms in that ecosystem within the context of *that* set of circumstances. Take an organism out of that set of circumstances and place it into another, and the story will be different. Hence, plants that have become rare or endangered in their original habitat may become weeds in other places. Within Australia, *Acacia baileyana*, the Cootamundra Wattle, is such a plant.

As environmentally concerned gardeners, the knowledge of nature's constant shifting and adjustment gives us opportunity. Although we do not have a large amount of land, we can be assured that whatever we do to welcome nature into our small patch, nature will find a way to make the most of. There are always doubters, and I have come across them during the writing of this book. Their main area of expertise is in finding reasons *not* to do things. Such people often want a perfect solution as justification for following a course of action. Their arguments are dense with buts and what ifs. I have no idea what a perfect solution is in this context, and there is no need for one.

Taking nature's qualities of opportunism and dynamism as our cue, the tiniest garden offers more scope than we can perceive for playing a part in maintaining the biosphere. All athletes do not win gold, nor do all musicians become concert pianists. Yet the contribution of the millions of non-gold winners and non-concert pianists to the worlds of sport and music are vastly more important in the lives of most of us than the contribution of the elite performers, for we may be those people ourselves. The elite in any sphere inspire us; they show us what is possible. In the same way, intact natural ecosystems show us what is possible, inspiring us with their innate and seemingly effortless brilliance to follow their lead in whatever way we can. Our gardens cannot do what they do, but that is not our aim.

One of the outstanding qualities of intact natural ecosystems that gardeners can take note of and copy is high levels of species diversity. Species richness is true of natural ecosystems even in harsh conditions such as deserts, seasides and alpine country. 'Poor soil', or aridity, or salt spray, or snow and ice do not deter nature from the great adventure of life with lists of buts and what ifs. Neither does size nor isolation. A frog will spawn in a puddle, a tree will grow in the crack of a rock, and palm trees and vines thrive around a spring in the desert. Nature is always ready to take a chance. Its experiments are not based on the recommendations of reports or the findings of studies. People are part of the matrix. We have the power to create ecosystems, as well as destroy them.

MAKING MINI-FORESTS

The Kayapo peoples of the Brazilian Amazon plant patches of forest in the savannah to help supply their needs for housing materials, food, medicine and other day-to-day items. These islands of forest within the grassland appear so natural that Westerners have assumed that they were a stage in the succession of savannah becoming jungle. They are not large-scale revegetation projects. No, they start off only a metre or two wide, a nucleus which gradually expands over time to cover a hectare or more.

The site selection is simple — usually a dish-shaped depression that will catch available moisture. The soil preparation is also simple, using a method akin to what we call no-dig gardening. They first make a compost heap of leaves and branches, leaving it to decay in the humid air on the life-filled soil. When it has partially decomposed, they crush it into fines and carry it to the chosen site, upon which they scatter soil from the nests of the world's great earthmovers, termites and ants. The compost is heaped into what we would call a 'raised bed' about 30 cm deep. Rainforest seedlings are transplanted into this rich nursery, usually during the wet season. Little maintenance is needed, and more plants are gradually added around the edges. As the mini-forest grows, natural seeding also takes place from the great genetic reservoir of the Amazon.

And just as plants and fungi move in of their own accord, so do birds and mammals, not to mention insects and the unseen billions of micro-organisms. A habitat garden has been grown, giving the Kayapo hunters easy access to prey. The garden is an island of biodiversity. It is independent, being grown from local species. It is a resource for the people who started it and for all the life forms that find it. Does size matter? No, size does not matter. It is plant diversity and local origin that matters. Science has provided evidence of the importance of plant diversity in a more clinical way, as we shall see.

The information we have from scientific research and our own observations tells us that environmental health is generally indicated by species richness, or biodiversity. That is, the more favourable conditions are for life, the more types of life there will be. It is circular, self-perpetuating: diverse life creates conditions that favour life.

A graphic illustration of this is evidence showing that levels of plant species diversity, rather than simply plant biomass, have a significant effect on the amount of carbon dioxide and nitrogen absorbed by an ecosystem. Carbon dioxide and nitrogen in the environment are both problematically on the increase due to human activity, while biodiversity is decreasing for the same reason. A study conducted in the US tested the hypothesis that low plant biodiversity reduces the efficiency of an ecosystem at absorbing excess carbon dioxide and nitrogen. During photosynthesis plants convert carbon dioxide into sugars and nitrogen into proteins. The research revealed that plots planted with many species absorbed about five times as much as plots planted with only a few species. That which is good for the Kayapo of the Amazon, it seems, is good for all of us.

BIODIVERSITY AND AGRICULTURE

Agricultural systems (and gardens) these days are usually based around growing only a few species. As we've seen, the modernisation of farming in England has caused dramatic changes to the biodiversity of the countryside as hedgerows have been removed and cropping cycles changed. In Australia, the experience of New England dieback showed that nature has critical biodiversity thresholds for self-maintenance— once these become too low, the process of species reduction increases, with nature even starting to self-destruct when the balance is lost.

Bearing in mind the domination of the rural landscape in the UK for many centuries, a report by Great Britain's peak organic organisation, the Soil Association, examined the relationship between biodiversity and organics.Published in 2000, it is titled 'The Biodiversity Benefits of Organic Farming' and was sponsored by The World Wildlife Fund (UK). Organic farming is usually promoted as a way of growing pesticide-free food without damaging the environment. This report takes the argument for organics one step further, examining not only how organics *prevents* damage, but showing that it has other far-reaching environmental benefits— by its very nature it enhances biodiversity. Seven thousand years of agriculture in the UK has created a landscape renowned for its picturesque beauty, interest and charm. Much of this beauty derives from the abundance of semi-natural habitats that are (or were) seamlessly interwoven throughout the farmlands. It appears there was a steady *increase* in biodiversity under the UK's traditional farming systems, peaking in the 1800s. *Farming was good for the environment.*

Rural biodiversity in the UK today, however, and no doubt in many parts of the world, is in crisis. Farmland covers at least 70 percent of the

UK, so biodiversity in the rural landscape represents a significant proportion of the nation's total opportunity to support biodiversity. And as the report points out, it is not only important to maintain diversity, but also its abundance. Statistics on farm bird numbers in recent years illustrate that the situation *is* a crisis. While birds from wild ecologies were showing some increases around 1999–2000, possibly due to mild winters, farm bird numbers briefly stabilised before continuing their downward trend. Dr Mark Avery, of the Royal Society for the Protection of Birds, in 2001 said, 'The UK's farmland birds are declining more rapidly than anywhere else in Europe.'[2]

Farm birds in the UK have declined by an average of 40 percent and several species by 80 percent. Tree sparrow numbers are a startling 90 percent less than in 1970. Remember that birds are an indicator for overall biodiversity, a point highlighted by the Birds on Farms Survey in Australia. In fact, the UK government tracks wild bird numbers for use as one of its primary indicators of sustainable development. The Australian survey complements the findings of the UK biodiversity report. Both find that high biodiversity is essential to agricultural sustainability and is a reflection of sound land management. The Australian Government Department of Environment and Heritage web page on biodiversity adds a further level of importance to the role of biodiversity on this Earth. It simply says that, 'Biodiversity underpins the processes that make life possible.'[3]

To achieve both diversity and abundance, the approaches that support biodiversity need to be widely practised. The research in both Australia and the UK/Europe shows that while conventional agriculture reduces biodiversity, organics enhances it. By going organic, farms also go beyond organics as they become rich ecologies which contribute to, rather than take from, environmental stability.

As gardeners we operate on a much smaller scale than farmers. The findings of the agricultural research, however, support the case for creating semi-natural habitats in our gardens. When you consider that the landscape is largely made up of nature reserves, farmland and residential areas, it is easier to see that all is linked. Our gardens fit into this overall picture and if they are havens for nature, the gaps between habitat areas reduce.

We know that globally, species diversity is in crisis. We have seen that the history of gardening is long, diverse and creative. There is much heritage and experience to draw on and develop. The relationship between people and their gardens has always reflected the needs and values of the times. The early walled, sanctuary gardens were refuges where the environment could be controlled in a world that was still largely wild. The sacred gardens and groves expressed deeply felt reverence and closeness to the intangible mysteries of the spirit. The practicality of food gardens evolved variously into high art, cradles of genetic variation and seemingly casual management of wilderness for food, as with the Kayapo. The aesthetics of paintings were brought to life by colourists such as Gertrude Jekyll and landscape visionaries as exemplified by Capability Brown. Here in the young gardening nation of Australia, naturalistic designers have paved the way to the acceptance and appreciation of our remarkable and diverse, but sadly oft-maligned, indigenous flora.

The time has come to merge gardens and the natural environment more purposefully and consciously than ever before. Gardeners are independent, innovative and hard working. As such, we are ideally placed to respond to the tragic loss of life and beauty that the biodiversity crisis really is. We have the ability to act on our values effectively and unselfishly, privileged as we are to have a space we call our garden.

THE GARDEN AS OASIS, NUCLEUS AND CONNECTION

As gardeners, examples of the creation of successful small-scale ecologies are an inspiration. From the patch-like forest gardens of the Kayapo to the organic farms of the UK, the message is that diverse, nature-welcoming sites become more diverse, and more nature-welcoming of their own accord. It is also of interest that the increases in biodiversity noticed on UK organic farms mostly occurred on properties that are akin to islands dotted within an ocean of conventionally farmed land, a limiting factor for biodiversity. In spite of this drawback, the rise in biodiversity on these farms is significant. As the area and proximity of organic farms increases, the biodiversity effects are likely to compound, spreading from these nuclei of nature. The same is true of each garden, albeit on a smaller scale.

By understanding and noticing the interactions that occur between your garden and the world outside the fence you can start to shift your gardening style in the ecological direction. Create a garden that welcomes nature and sustains the biosphere. Your creation will be both an oasis and a nucleus for the biodiversity that sustains all life on Earth. And as we have seen, in reality there is no isolation. All is linked and all is shared.

ENDNOTES

CHAPTER 1
1 Gibbons, B & L 1996 (1988), *Creating a Wildlife Garden*, Chancellor Press, 1996, London, p. 10

CHAPTER 2
1 Howard (Sir) A 1979 (1943), *An Agricultural Testament*, Rodale Press, PA, pp. 9-10
2 Jekyll, G as quoted in Kellaway, D (ed) 1997, *The Illustrated Virago Book of Women Gardeners*, Hodder Headline, Sydney, p. 11
3 ibid., p. 84
4 Conder, J 2002 (1893), *Landscape Gardening in Japan*, Kodansha International, Tokyo, p. 21
5 ibid., pp 21 & 31
6 Walling, E as quoted in Barrett, M (ed) 1985 (1948), *A Gardener's Log*, Anne O'Donovan, Hawthorn, Victoria, p. 72
7 Barrett, M (ed) 1985 (1948), *A Gardener's Log*, Anne O'Donovan, Hawthorn, Victoria, p. 76
8 Ford, G 1999, Gordon Ford: the Natural Australian Garden, Bloomings Books, Melbourne, p.3
9 ibid.
10 ibid., p. xi
11 Thompson, P 2002, *Australian Planting Design*, Lothian Books, Melbourne, p. x
12 Timms, P 1999, *The Nature of Gardens*, Allen & Unwin, Sydney, p. 261

CHAPTER 3
1 Suzuki, D & Knudtson, P 1992, *The Wisdom of the Elders*, Allen & Unwin, Sydney, p. 43

CHAPTER 4
1 Attenborough, D 1995, *The Private Life of Plants*, BBC Books, London, pp. 96-97
2 ibid, p. 124
3 ibid., p. 119

CHAPTER 5
1 NSW Parks and Wildlife Service 2004, 'NPWS Asks for Community Help to Control Spread of Glory Lily', media release, 9 January, http://www.nationalparks.nsw.gov.au/npws.nsf/Content/media_120104_glory_lily
2 Low, T 1999, *Feral Future*, Viking, Ringwood, Vic., p. 219
3 Reinikka, M A 1972, *A History of the Orchid*, University of Miami Press, Miami, USA
4 ibid.
5 Fauna and Flora International Indigenous Propagation Project (Turkey): The Wild Bulb Trade, http://www.floralocale.org/resources/propagation/FFIIPP.html
6 Karingal Consultants, 1997 'Review of the Commercial Domestic Trade in Long-Lived Native Plants', abstract of a report written for Environment Australia, November, http://www.deh.gov.au/biodiversity/trade-use/wild-harvest/plants/plants-trade.html
7 Robbins, C & Luna, RTB 2003, 'Prickly Trade: Trade and Conservation of Chihuahuan Desert Cacti', report written for TRAFFIC North America, Washington
8 ibid.
9 2003, 'Cactus Poaching, Legal Harvesting A Growing Threat to Chihuahuan Desert Cacti', press release, Switzerland, 10 January, http://www.traffic.org/news/press-releases/cactus_poaching.html

Endnotes

Endnotes

CHAPTER 6

1. Buchanan, R 1989, *Bush Regeneration — Recovering Australian Landscapes*, TAFE Student Learning Publications, NSW, p. 217
2. Dawson, K J as quoted in Francis, M & Hester, Jr. RT (eds) 1990, *The Meaning of Gardens: Idea, Place and Action*, MIT Press Cambridge, Massachusetts, p. 138
3. Carson, R 1962, *Silent Spring*, Crest Books, New York, p. 57
4. Baumgartner, K 2004, 'Alternatives to Pre-emergent Herbicide', Newsletter of the University of California Sustainable Agriculture Research and Education Program, vol 16 no.1-2, summer 2004, p. 8, www.sarep.ucdavis.edu/newsltr/v16n1/v16n1.pdf
5. 1991, 'Garden Birds Survey', online document, Bird Observers Club of Australia, www.birdobservers.org.au

CHAPTER 7

1. Carson, R 1962, *Silent Spring*, Crest Books, New York, p. 159

CHAPTER 8

1. Barrett, J & Ford, H 1993, *Birds on Farms: A New England Perspective*, Greening Australia, Armidale, NSW, p. 1
2. Barrett, G 2000, *Birds on Farms: Ecological Management for Agricultural Sustainability*, Birds Australia, Victoria, p. ii

CHAPTER 9

1. Carson, R 1962, *Silent Spring*, Crest Books, New York, p. 97
2. The website developed by the Nursery Industry Association of Australia with information to help gardeners select fauna-friendly plants suitable to their region is at www.floraforfauna.com.au

CHAPTER 10

1. The Green Revolution was based around replacing traditionally grown varieties with high-yielding hybrid grains.
2. Solomon, S 2002, *Growing Vegetables South of Australia*, Steve Solomon, Tasmania, p. 178
3. The network can be contacted via its website at www.seedsavers.net
4. Tokar, B (ed.) 2001, *Redesigning Life?: the Worldwide Challenge to Genetic Engineering*, Scribe Publications, Carlton North, Vic., p.6
5. CSIRO Ozone depletion information sheet at www.csiro.gov.au

CHAPTER 11

1. Carson, R 1962, *Silent Spring*, Crest Books, New York, p. 44
2. Howard (Sir) A 1979 (1943), *An Agricultural Testament*, Rodale Press, PA, p. 2

CHAPTER 12

1. Walling, E quoted in Barrett, M (ed) 1985 (1948), *A Gardener's Log*, Anne O'Donovan, Hawthorn, Vic., p. 123
2. Thompson, P 2002, *Australian Planting Design*, Lothian Books, Melbourne, p. 39
3. Barrett, G 2000, *Birds on Farms: Ecological Management for Agricultural Sustainability*, Birds Australia, Vic., p. iii
4. Walling, E quoted in Barrett, M (ed) 1985, *A Gardener's Log*, Anne O'Donovan, Hawthorn, Vic., p. 146
5. Grant, J (ed) 1997, *The Nest Box Book*, The Gould League, Australia
6. Barrett, G 2000, *Birds on Farms: Ecological Management for Agricultural Sustainability*, Birds Australia, Vic., p. xiii
7. Hill, R (Minister for Environment and Heritage) 1996, 'Native Grasslands Receive Recognition',

media release, 1 August, Australian Government,
http://www.deh.gov.au/minister/env/96/mr1aug.html
8　'Problems Associated with Traditional Landscaping', US National Wildlife Federation,
http://www.nwf.org/backyardwildlifehabitat/problems.cfm
9　Coleby-Williams, J 2000, 'Getting Exuberant', *Organic Gardener*, Summer 2000, p. 32
10　Barrett, G 2000, *Birds on Farms: Ecological Management for Agricultural Sustainability*,
Birds Australia, Vic., p. xii
11　ibid.

CHAPTER 13
1　Thompson, P 2002, *Australian Planting Design*, Lothian Books, Melbourne, p. 43
2　Freudenberger, D & Harvey, J 2003, *Assessing the Benefits of Vegetation Enhancement for Biodiversity: a Draft Framework*, a report for Environment Australia and the Biodiversity Benefits Task Group CSIRO Sustainable Ecosystems, Environment Australia, May, p. 18
3　ibid., p. 19
4　ibid., p. 22
5　Grant, J (ed) 1997, *The Nest Box Book*, The Gould League, Australia

CHAPTER 14
1　Solomon, S 2002, *Growing Vegetables South of Australia*, Steve Solomon, Tasmania, p. 5
2　www.aussieseedsaverscatalogue.net
3　Suzuki, D & Knudtson, P 1992, *The Wisdom of the Elders*, Allen & Unwin, Sydney, p.106

CHAPTER 15
1　Carson, R 1962, *Silent Spring*, Crest Books, New York, p. 218
2　Avery, M as quoted in BBC News Online, 19 December 2001
3　The Department of Environment and Heritage webpage on diversity is at
www.deh.gov.au/biodiversity

OTHER REFERENCES

www.acehardware.com/info
www.csu.edu.au/research/farrer
www.eartheasy.com
www.rightlivelihood.org/recip/chipko.htm

Azeez, G 2000, '*The Biodiversity Benefits of Organic Farming*', a report for Soil Association, Bristol, UK

Bormann, F H, Balmori, D & Geballe, G T 1993, *Redesigning the American Lawn: A Search for Environmental Harmony*, Yale University Press, Newhaven

Kipling, R 1993 (1901), *Kim*, Wordsworth Editions, Hertfordshire

Suzuki, D & McConnell, A 1999, *The Sacred Balance*, Allen & Unwin, Sydney

Suzuki, D. 2002, *Good News for a Change*, Allen & Unwin, Sydney

Walters, B. 2003, 'Australian Plants', online table, Society for Growing Australian Plants (ASGAP), at
http://farrer.riv.csu.edu.au/ASGAP/APOL31/sep03-2.

Index